Principles of
Writing
Research
Papers

Professor J. D. Lester (1935–2006) was a distinguished scholar of literature and mythology who taught for 30 years at Austin Peay State University in Clarksville, Tennessee. With over 33 published books to his credit, he continues to be best known for his hallmark research textbook, *Writing Research Papers: A Complete Guide*. Now in its twelfth edition, this best-selling text has been used and praised by nearly three million students and instructors alike.

James D. Lester, Jr. is an instructor of composition at Clayton State University in Morrow, Georgia. His 25 years of experience as a classroom teacher at Mount Zion High School in Jonesboro, Georgia have helped create a practical and manageable guide to direct learners through the research process. Professor Lester earned his Ph.D. in English Education from Georgia State University in Atlanta, Georgia.

Principles of
Writing
Research
Papers

Second Edition

James D. Lester

James D. Lester, Jr.

PENGUIN ACADEMICS

PEARSON
Longman

New York   San Francisco   Boston
London   Toronto   Sydney   Tokyo   Singapore   Madrid
Mexico City   Munich   Paris   Cape Town   Hong Kong   Montreal

Publisher: Joseph Opiela
Senior Marketing Manager: Sandra McGuire
Production Manager: Denise Phillip
Project Coordination, Text Design, and Electronic Page Makeup:
   Electronic Publishing Services Inc., NYC
Senior Cover Design Manager/Cover Designer: Nancy Danahy
Cover Image: © Getty Inc.
Senior Manufacturing Buyer: Dennis J. Para
Printer and Binder: R. R. Donnelley & Sons
Cover Printer: Phoenix Color Corporation

For more information about the Penguin Academic series, please contact us by mail at Longman Publishers, attn. Marketing Department, 1185 Avenue of the Americas, 25th Floor, New York, NY 10036, or by e-mail at www.ablongman.com

For permission to use copyrighted material, grateful acknowledgment is made to the copyright holders on p. 255, which is hereby made part of this copyright page.

Library of Congress Cataloging-in-Publication Data
Lester, James D.
   Principles of writing research papers / James D. Lester, Jr. — 2nd ed.
      p. cm.
   Includes index.
   Rev. ed. of: Principles of writing research papers / James D. Lester, Sr.,
   James D. Lester, Jr. 2003.
   ISBN 0-321-42610-X
   1. Report writing—Handbooks, manuals, etc.   2. Research—Handbooks,
manuals, etc.   I. Title.
LB2369.L393 2007
808'.02—dc22

                                                            2006009657

Please visit us at www.ablongman.com

ISBN 0-321-42610-X

3 4 5 6 7 8 9 10–DOC–09

Contents

CHAPTER EIGHT Drafting the Paper in an Academic Style 110

Preface

This second edition of *Principles of Writing Research Papers* has several new features to serve students and instructors in first-year composition courses as well as upper-level researchers. In brief, it provides

- well-focused information on electronic research.
- help with electronic presentations.
- a new focus on critical reading with an emphasis on academic integrity.
- thorough discussions on composing from sources.
- information about writing methods in the various disciplines.
- current information from the most recent style guides.
- new student papers.
- an ancillary package.

Electronic Research

The text explores the new aspects of library research. It spotlights the academic databases that can be accessed only through a library's electronic system. It encourages controlled Internet searches and sets guidelines for acceptable academic sites. It helps students conduct field research by providing information about interviews, questionnaires, and correspondence by e-mail and Web conferencing. The text provides students with a comprehensive list, by discipline, of important reference tools.

Electronic Presentations

The *Principles* guide has a complete chapter for students who wish to present their research project electronically. The chapter explains the various methods for developing the research paper with slide presentations, Web pages, Web sites, and digital graphics. It also explains the methods for delivering the paper by e-mail, zip drives, CD-ROM, and Web sites.

An Emphasis on Academic Integrity

Electronic retrieval has made plagiarism a pervasive problem, so the authors have created a new chapter, short but to the point, on what constitutes plagiarism. The same passage is reproduced repeatedly to demonstrate the differences between writing that cites sources properly and writing that fails the test of plagiarism in blatant and subtle ways.

Focus on Critical Reading

Chapters 6 and 7 now give invaluable tips to students on such matters as identifying the best sources, evaluating them for relevancy, authority, and accuracy, and—just as important—creating notes that summarize, quote, and paraphrase effectively and to a point. This section also shows students how to use their notes to build an annotated bibliography and a review of the literature on a narrowed topic.

Composing with Sources

The *Principles* guide helps students find good sources, create effective notes in a variety of fashions, and then—most important of all—blend those sources into an effective piece of writing, one in which the student's voice is not lost, yet in which the sources provide support and confirmation of key and theories. Thus, Chapter 10, on blending sources for an academic style, is one that instructors not only assign but walk the students through.

Keeping Current to the Latest Standards

The default style for textual instruction in the text is the MLA style for students and instructors in literature and composition. Hence, it conforms to the MLA handbook, *MLA Handbook for Writers of Research Papers*, 6th edition, 2003.

New Student Papers

To demonstrate MLA style, the text contains three papers:

"Annotated Bibliography," by Norman Levenson

"Gender Communication: A Review of the Literature," by Kaci Holz

"Listening to Hamlet: The Soliloquies," by Melinda Mosier

Acknowledgments

For their encouragement and devotion to this project, our love goes to our family members: Martha, Mark, Debbie, Caleb, and Sarah.

James D. Lester, Jr.
jameslester@mail.clayton.edu
Morrow, GA

CHAPTER ONE

FINDING A
SCHOLARLY TOPIC

You will seldom go in search of a topic so much as you will focus a pre-existing general subject, one given to you by the instructor or one that you have wanted to explore but had no reason for doing so. As you move from class to class, keep your focus on the issues of each course. A health class might suggest this topic to somebody who smokes and who has a family to worry about: "Secondhand Smoke: Is It a Firsthand Danger?" A literature instructor might require you to explore Nathaniel Hawthorne's fiction, which is nineteenth-century material, but you can make it contemporary: "Hester Prynne in the Twenty-First Century: Who Wears the Scarlet Letter Today?" These topics meet the expectations of composition instructors as well as those of instructors in health, sociology, political science, education, and many other disciplines. Consider the following list of possible topics:

EDUCATION:	The Visually Impaired: Options for Classroom Participation
POLITICAL SCIENCE:	The Impact of the Presidential Electoral College
HEALTH:	The Effects of Chemicals on Athletic Performance
SOCIOLOGY:	Parents Who Lie to Their Children: Psychological Consequences

1a Generating Ideas and Focusing the Subject

You can generate ideas for research and focus on the issues with a number of techniques:

- Relate your personal ideas to a scholarly problem.
- Talk with others.
- Examine electronic sources.
- Read textbooks and reference books.

Relating Your Personal Ideas to a Scholarly Problem

Draw on yourself for ideas, keep a research journal, ask yourself questions, and get comfortable with new terminology.

Personal Ideas   Contemplate personal issues to generate ideas worthy of investigation. At a quiet time, begin writing, questioning, and pushing on the various buttons of your mind for your feelings and attitudes. The research paper should reflect your thinking in response to the sources. It should not merely report what others have said. If possible, combine a personal interest with one aspect of your academic studies:

ACADEMIC SUBJECT:	Health, especially sports medicine
PERSONAL INTEREST:	Skiing
POSSIBLE TOPICS:	Protecting the Knees
	Therapy for Strained Muscles
	Skin Treatments

You might also consider social issues that affect you and your family:

ACADEMIC SUBJECT:	Education
PERSONAL INTEREST:	The behavior of my child in school
POSSIBLE TOPICS:	Calming Children Who Are Hyperactive
	Should Schoolchildren Take Medicine to Calm Their Hyperactivity?

Your cultural background can prompt you toward detailed research into your roots, your culture, and the mythology and history of your ethnic background:

ACADEMIC SUBJECT:	History
ETHNIC BACKGROUND:	Native Americans
PERSONAL INTEREST:	History of the Apache tribes
POSSIBLE TOPIC:	The Indian Wars from the Native American's Point of View

A Research Journal Unlike a diary of personal thoughts about your daily activities or a journal of creative ideas, such as poems, stories, and scenarios, the research journal enables you to list issues, raise questions, create notes, and develop pieces of free writing. In fact, you should build the journal primarily with **free writing** as well as **keywords and phrases** that come to mind. These establish primary categories for your research. One student listed several terms and phrases about the use of midwives in the rural Southeastern mountains:

natural childbirth	disinfectants	recovery time
prenatal care	medicines	delivery
hardships	complications	sterilization
delivery problems	deaths	cost

In her research journal, she began writing notes on these topics, like this:

The cost of delivery by a midwife in the mother's home differs so greatly from the cost of a doctor and a hospital that we can only appreciate the plight of those using this procedure.

The research journal is also a place for preliminary outlining to find the major and minor issues, as shown here:

Midwives in the Rural Southeast Mountains

Preparation:	Delivery:	Recovery:	Cost:
prenatal care	natural	after delivery	one fee
sterilization	childbirth	recovery time	
disinfectants	medicines	deaths	
	delivery		
	techniques		

Questions   Asking questions in your research journal can focus your attention on primary issues, and your subsequent notes in answer to the questions can launch your investigation. For example, having read Henry Thoreau's essay "Civil Disobedience," one writer posed these questions:

```
What is civil disobedience?

Is dissent legal? Is it moral? Is it patriotic?

Is dissent a liberal activity? Conservative?

Should the government encourage or stifle dissent?

Is passive resistance effective?
```

Answering the questions can lead the writer to a central issue or argument, such as "Civil Disobedience: Shaping Our Nation."

Academic disciplines across the curriculum invite questions that might provoke a variety of answers and give focus to the subject, as with "sports gambling."

ECONOMICS:
: Does sports gambling benefit a college's athletic budget? Does it benefit the national economy?

PSYCHOLOGY:
: What is the effect of gambling on the mental attitude of the college athlete who knows that huge sums hang in the balance on his/her performance?

HISTORY:
: Does gambling on sporting events have an identifiable tradition?

SOCIOLOGY:
: What compulsion in human nature prompts people to gamble on athletic prowess?

POLITICAL SCIENCE:
: What laws exist in this state for the control of illegal sports gambling? Are they enforced?

Terminology   Each discipline has its own terminology. For example, in researching a paper on retail marketing you might learn to refer to "the demographics" of a "target audience." In psychological research, you might learn to use the phrases "control group" and "experimental group." One student found essential words for her paper on diabetes:

diabetes	diabetes mellitus	glucose
insulin	metabolize	hyperglycemia
pancreas	ketoacidosis	ketones

She learned the meaning of each term and applied it properly in her paper, giving her work a scholarly edge.

Talking with Others to Find and Refine the Topic

Sometime early in your project, go outside yourself to get feedback on your possible topic and its issues. You can accomplish this task with personal interviews, participation in e-mail discussion groups, and on a limited basis in Internet chat forums. Moreover, do not hesitate to speak with your instructor about your topic or a research librarian at you school's media center for assistance in selecting a direction for your study.

Personal Interview   A personal interview, either face to face, by telephone, or by e-mail, allows you to consult with experts and people in your community for ideas and reactions to your subject. Explore a subject for key ideas while having coffee or a soda with a colleague, relative, or work associate.

> **HINT:** Casual conversations that contribute to your understanding of the subject need not be documented. However, a formal interview or an in-depth discussion with an expert demands credit in your text and a citation in the Works Cited page at the end of your paper.

Local E-mail Discussion Group   Many instructors establish e-mail discussion groups for their courses to meet the demands of special interest groups. These discussion boards are popular with online courses, especially those using the Blackboard software for course management. These are private sites reserved for class members and the instructors, so they focus on the specific interests of the group. Thus, you can get input from your peers as well as your instructor, and you can make pertinent queries about your subject matter.

Internet Discussion Group During an online chat conversation, you might find a few ideas on your topic; however, *heed this warning*: participants use fictitious names, provide unreliable sources, are highly opinionated in most instances, and therefore *they cannot be quoted in your paper.* The best you might gain is marginal insight into the ideas of people who are often eccentric and who hide behind their anonymity.

Using Electronic Sources

The library is your best source for electronic articles. Start with the library's academic databases and its electronic book catalog. After that, search the World Wide Web. You might also examine CDs and videotapes.

Library Databases Go to the reliable databases available through your library, such as InfoTrac, PsychINFO, UMI ProQuest, Electric Library, and EBSCOhost. You can reach these from remote locations at home or the dorm room by connecting to your library with your personal identification number. The library has monitored Internet sites filtered by editorial boards and peer review. Many articles on these databases appeared first in print. In many cases, you can read an abstract of the article before reading the full text. You can also print the article without going into the stacks. However, libraries vary in their access to electronic databases, so be sure to consult with the reference librarians.

Electronic Book Catalogs Use your library's computerized index to find books, film, DVD holdings, and similar items. Enter a key word, such as "George W. Bush," and you will get a listing of all books by and about the President. The book catalog will not index the titles to articles in magazines and journals, but it will tell you which periodicals are housed in the library and whether they are housed in a printed volume, on microforms, or an electronic database (see immediately above). Instructors will want you to consult books during your research, so follow these steps:

1. Enter a topic that will generate a reasonably sized list, such as "nutrition."

2. Examine the various entries in detail, starting with the most recent to find books related to your topic.

3. In the stacks find and examine each book for relevance. *Tip:* While in the stacks examine nearby books, for they will likely treat the same subject.

World Wide Web   Articles on the Internet offer ideas about how other people approach the subject, and these ideas can help you refine your topic. Use the subject directory on a browser, such as Google, to probe from a general topic to specific articles (Health > Diseases > Blood disorders > Anemia). Use a keyword search when you already have a specific topic. Thus, entering the keyword "anemia" will send you immediately to various Web articles. See Chapter 3, pages 45–50, for more about searching the Internet.

CD-ROM, DVD, VHS   *Encarta, Electronic Classical Library, Compton's Interactive Encyclopedia,* and other reference diskettes are available. Browsing at one of these sources will give you a good feel for the depth and strength of the subject and suggest a list of narrowed topics. Check with a librarian, a department office, and your instructor for disks and videos in a specialty area, such as mythology, poetry, or American history. These media forms can sometimes be found in local bookstores or purchased over the Internet.

Using Textbooks and Reference Books

Dipping into your own textbooks can reward you with topic ideas, and a trip to the library to examine books and indexes in the reference room can also be beneficial.

Library Books and Textbooks   With your working topic in hand, do some exploratory reading. Carefully examine the **titles** of books, noting key terminology. Search a book's **table of contents** for topics. A history book on the American Civil War might display these headings:

The Clash of Amateur Armies

Real Warfare Begins

The Navies

Confederate High-Water Mark

If any heading looks interesting to you, go to the book's **index** for additional headings, such as this sample:

Jefferson Davis, President of the Confederate States
    evacuates Richmond, 574, 576
    foreign relations, 250, 251
    imprisonment of, 567
    inauguration, 52–53
    peace proposals, 564–65

Perhaps the topic on peace proposals will spur your interest in all peace proposals—that is, how nations end wars and send their troops home safely.

Reference Books   If you do not have access to an electronic database, the printed indexes, such as the *Readers' Guide to Periodical Literature*, *Bibliographic Index*, and *Humanities Index*, categorize and subdivide topics by alphabetical order. Searching under a keyword or phrase usually leads to a list of critical articles on the subject, and studying the titles might suggest a narrowed topic. For example, looking under the heading "Single Mothers" might produce several possible topics, such as "Welfare Moms," "Single Motherhood," or "Racial Differentials in Child Support."

> ■ **HINT:** Topic selection goes beyond choosing a general category (e.g., "single mothers"). It includes finding a research-provoking issue or question, such as "The foster parent program seems to have replaced the orphanage system. Has it been effective?" That is, you need to take a stand, adopt a belief, or begin asking questions. For more information, see section 1c, "Drafting a Research Proposal."

1b Writing a Thesis, Enthymeme, or Hypothesis

Usually, one central statement controls an essay's direction and content, so as early as possible, begin thinking in terms of a controlling idea. Each type shown below has a separate mission:

- A **thesis statement** advances a conclusion the writer will defend: *Contrary to what some philosophers have advanced, human beings have always participated in wars.*

- An **enthymeme** uses a *because* clause to make a claim the writer will defend: *There has never been a "noble savage," as such, because even prehistoric human beings fought frequent wars for numerous reasons.*

- A **hypothesis** is a theory that must be tested in the laboratory, in the literature, and/or by field research to prove its validity: *Human beings are motivated by biological instincts toward the physical overthrow of perceived enemies.*

Each type is discussed next.

Thesis Statement

A thesis sentence expands your topic into a scholarly proposal, one that you will try to prove and defend in your paper. It does not state the obvious, such as "Langston Hughes was a great poet from Harlem." That sentence cannot provoke an academic discussion because readers know that any published poet has talent. The writer must isolate one issue by finding a critical focus, such as this one:

```
Langston Hughes used a controversial vernacular
language that paved the way for later artists, even
today's rap musicians.
```

This sentence advances an idea that the writer can develop fully and defend with evidence. The writer has made a connection between the subject, *Langston Hughes*, and the focusing agent, *vernacular language*. A general thesis might state:

```
Certain nutritional foods can prevent disease.
```

But note how your interest in an academic area can color the thesis:

HEALTH: ```Nutritional foods may be a promising addition to the diet of people wishing to avoid certain diseases.```

ECONOMICS: ```Nutritional foods can become an economic weapon in the battle against rising health care costs.```

HISTORY: `Other civilizations, including`
`primitive tribes, have known about`
`food's nutritional values for cen-`
`turies. We can learn from their`
`knowledge.`

A thesis sets in motion the writer's examination of specific ideas the study will explore and defend. Thus, when confronted by a general topic, such as "television," adjust it to an academic interest, as with "Video replays have improved football officiating but slowed the game" or "Video technology has enhanced arthroscopic surgery."

Your thesis is not your conclusion or your answer to a problem. Rather, it anticipates your conclusion by setting in motion the examination of facts and pointing the reader toward the special idea of your paper, which you save for the conclusion.

Enthymeme

Some of your instructors might want the research paper to develop an argument as expressed in an enthymeme, which consists of two parts: a claim supported with a because clause. However, you need to understand that the enthymeme has a structure that depends on one or more unstated assumptions.

> `Hyperactive children need medication because ADHD`
> `is a medical disorder, not a behavioral problem.`

The claim that hyperactive children need medication is supported by the stated reason that the condition is a medical problem, not one of behavior. This writer must address the unstated assumption that medication alone will solve the problem.

> `Participating in one of the martial arts, such as`
> `Tae Kwan Do, is good for children because it`
> `promotes self-discipline.`

The claim that one organized sporting activity is good for children rests on the value of self-discipline. Unstated is the assumption that one sport, the martial arts, is good for children in other areas of development, such as physical conditioning. The writer might also address other issues, such as aggression or a combat mentality.

Hypothesis

A hypothesis is a theory that must be tested to prove its validity and an assumption advanced for the purpose of argument or investigation. Here's an example:

> Discrimination against girls and young women in the
> classroom, known as <u>shortchanging</u>, harms the
> chances of women to develop fully academically.

This statement could lead to a theoretical study if the student cites literature on the ways in which teachers shortchange students. A professional educator, on the other hand, would probably conduct extensive research in many classroom settings to defend the hypothesis with scientific observation.

Sometimes the hypothesis is *conditional:*

> Our campus has a higher crime rate than other state
> colleges.

This assertion on a conditional state of being could be tested by statistical comparison. At other times the hypothesis is *relational:*

> Class size affects the number of written
> assignments given by writing instructors.

This type of hypothesis claims that as one variable changes, so does another, or that something is more or less than another. It could be tested by examining and correlating class size and assignments.

At other times, the researcher produces a *causal hypothesis:*

> A child's choice of a toy is determined by
> television commercials.

This causal hypothesis assumes the mutual occurrence of two factors and asserts that one factor is responsible for the other. The student who is a parent could conduct research to prove or disprove the supposition.

Thus, your paper, motivated by a hypothesis, might be a theoretical examination of the literature or field study on such topics as the diet of migrating geese, the yield of one species of hybrid corn, or the behavior of children as they watch violence on television. See also pages 53–62 for more information on field research.

CHECKLIST NARROWING A GENERAL SUBJECT
             INTO A WORKING TOPIC

Unlike a general subject, a focused topic should:

- Examine one significant issue, not a broad subject.
- Argue from a thesis sentence, enthymeme, or hypothesis.
- Address a knowledgeable reader and carry that reader to another plateau of knowledge.
- Have a serious purpose, one that demands analysis of the issues, argues from a position, and explains complex details.
- Meet the expectations of the instructor and conform to the course requirements.

1c Drafting a Research Proposal

A research proposal helps clarify and focus a research project. It comes in two forms: (1) a short paragraph that identifies the project for approval of your instructor, or (2) several pages that give background information, your rationale for conducting the study, a review of the literature, your methods, and the thesis, enthymeme, or hypothesis you plan to defend.

Writing a Short Research Proposal

A short proposal identifies five essential ingredients of your project:

1. The specific topic.
2. The purpose of the paper (explain, analyze, argue).
3. The intended audience (general or specialized).
4. Your position as the writer (informer, interpreter, evaluator, reviewer).
5. The preliminary thesis sentence or opening hypothesis.

One writer developed this brief proposal:

```
The world is running out of fresh water while we
sip our Evian. However, the bottled water craze
signals something—we don't trust our fresh tap
```

water. We have an emerging crisis on our hands, and some authorities forecast world wars over water rights. The issue of water touches almost every facet of our lives, from religious rituals and food supply to disease and political instability. We might frame this hypothesis: Water will soon replace oil as the economic resource most treasured by nations of the world. However, that assertion would prove difficult to defend and may not be true at all. Rather, we need to look elsewhere, at human behavior, and at human responsibility for preserving the environment for our children. Accordingly, this paper will examine
(1) the issues with regard to supply and demand,
(2) the political power struggles that may emerge, and
(3) the ethical implications for those who control the world's scattered supply of fresh water.

Writing a Detailed Research Proposal

A long proposal presents specific details concerning the project. It has more depth and length than the short proposal shown above. The long proposal should include some or all of the following elements:

1. *Cover page* with the title of the project, your name, and the person or agency to whom you are submitting the proposal (see page 116 for details on writing titles and pages 166–167 for the form of a title page).

2. An *abstract* that summarizes your project in 50 to 100 words (see pages 93–94 for an example).

3. A *purpose statement* with your *rationale* for the project (see the short proposal above for an example). Use *explanation* to review and itemize factual data. One writer explained how diabetes can be managed. Use *analysis* to classify parts of the subject and to investigate each one in depth. Use *persuasion* to question general attitudes about a

problem and then to affirm new theories, advance a solution, recommend a course of action, or—in the least—invite the reader into an intellectual dialog.

4. A *statement of qualification* that explains your experience and perhaps the special qualities you bring to the project (i.e., you are the parent of a child with ADHD). If you have no experience with the subject, you can omit the statement of qualification.

5. A *review of the literature* that surveys the articles and books you have examined in your preliminary work (see pages 98–109 for an explanation and an example of a review of literature).

1d Establishing a Schedule

The steps for producing a research paper have remained fundamental for many years. You will do well to follow them, even to the point of setting deadlines on the calendar for each step. In the spaces below, write dates to remind yourself when deadlines should be met.

_____ *Topic approved by the instructor.* The topic must have a built-in question or argument so that you can interpret an issue and cite the opinions found in the source materials.

_____ *Reading and creating a working bibliography.* Preliminary reading establishes the basis for your research, helping you to discover the quantity and quality of available sources.

_____ *Organizing.* A research journal will indicate the direction of your work. You might also consider organizing with a formal outline. In either case, see Chapter 5.

_____ *Creating notes.* Begin entering notes in your research journal, either in a notebook or in a computer file. Write plenty of notes and collect a supply of photocopied pages.

_____ *Drafting the paper.* During your writing, let your instructor scan the draft to give you feedback and guidance. See chapter 8 for more details on drafting in an academic style.

_____ *Writing a list of your references.* You will need to list the various sources used in your study. Chapter 11 provides documentation guidelines for MLA style.

_____ *Revision and Proofreading.* Be conscientious about examining the manuscript and making final corrections. Chapter 9 will give you tips on formatting, revision, and editing.

_____ *Submitting the manuscript.* Like all writers, you will need at some point to "publish" the paper—on paper, on a disk, on a CD-ROM, or on your own Web site.

Your Research Project

1. Develop a short research proposal for your proposed research project as explained in section 1c. Submit your proposal to your instructor for approval.

2. Use the schedule for section 1d as a guide to begin working on your research project. Some instructors will give you a timetable for the project. You may also want to consult individually with your instructor for assistance, including the date for submission of the final project.

CHAPTER TWO

LIBRARY RESEARCH

With a refined topic in hand, you can begin research in three different places—the library, the Internet, and the field. The next three chapters will explore these options.

2a Finding Sources with Your Library Access

You can begin your research from your apartment, your dorm room, one of the computer labs, or the library itself. All you need is online access to the library with your student identification. Your initial strategy will normally include three stages: the initial search to gauge the academic atmosphere for your subject, fine-tuning your focus for in-depth searching, and building your own electronic journal with a working bibliography, printouts, and downloaded items. In addition, it will pay dividends for you to stroll through your library to identify its various sections and make mental notes of the types of information available there.

Begin your initial search at the library's electronic book catalog and electronic databases because they will:

- Show the availability of source materials with diverse opinions.

- Provide a beginning set of reference citations, abstracts, full-text articles, and books, some with full text for printing or downloading.

- Help to restrict the subject and narrow your focus.

- Give an overview of the subject by showing how others have discussed it.

> **HINT:** Today's college library not only houses academic books and periodicals, it connects you by the Internet to thousands of academic resources that you cannot reach any other way. So when you visit your college library in person or by computer link, you are assured of getting sources that have been reviewed carefully and judged worthy of your time and interest. This differs from a general Internet browser, which cannot access the scholarship material at the academic sites. A general browser, such as Google or Lycos, might send you anywhere. The library's databases will send you to reputable sources.

2b Using the Library's Electronic Book Catalog

Your library's computerized catalog probably has a name such as LIBNET, FELIX, ACORN, or UTSEARCH. It serves as your primary source for several items.

Books

The catalog lists every book in the library filed by subject, author, and title along with the call number, its location in the stacks, and its availability, as shown in this example:

Research: Successful Approaches Elaine R. Monsen, ed.

Subjects: Nutrition research / Dietetics research

Location: General Book Collection, Level 3

Call number: TX367.R46 2003

Status: Available

In many cases, clicking on the title gives you an abstract of the book. Sometimes the library's catalog will provide access to electronic books on the World Wide Web, as shown by this example, which provides a URL hyperlink:

Nutrition in Early Life [electronic resource]

Edited by Jane B. Morgan and John W. T. Dickerson

Internet access: http://www.netLibrary.com/
urlapi.asp?action=summary&v=1&bookid=79551

Journals

The catalog includes references to journals in bound volumes physically housed at the library or electronically on the Internet, with links for accessing them.

Journal of Nutrition Education and Behavior

Availability: Periodicals Collection, Level 1

This journal is available at the library.

The American Journal of Clinical Nutrition [electronic resource]

Internet access: Full text available from Highwire Press (Free Journals)

http://highwire.standford.edu/lists/freeart.dtl

This journal, not housed in the library, is accessed only by clicking on the hyperlink. We discuss this feature in the next section, 2c.

Internet Sites

The catalog includes hyperlinks to Web sites the librarians have identified as excellent academic sources, such as this government document:

Food and Nutrition [electronic resource]

Washington, DC: Food and Nutrition Service, U.S. Dept. of Agriculture

Internet access: Full text available from Health and Wellness Resource
http://morris.lib.apsu.edu/rpa/webauth.exe?rs= wellness

Reference Books

The electronic catalog also lists reference books. It indexes by call number those housed in the library. Those available online have hypertext links.

Essay and General Literature Index

H. W. Wilson Company

Location: Reference Stacks, Level 2

Status: Available

Call number: A13 .E752

Social Sciences [electronic resource]

Internet access: Full text available from Columbia International Affairs Online http://www.ciaonet.org/

Archives

Archival research takes you into past literature so you can trace developing issues and ideas on a subject.

Archives of Dermatology [electronic resource]

Internet access: Full text available from InfoTrac
    http://morris.lib.apsu.edu/rpa/webauth.exe?rs= eai

Bibliographies

Bibliographies list the works by a writer or the works about a subject. They give you access to the titles of articles and books on your topic, usually up to a certain date, as shown in this next resource.

Bibliography of Tobacco-Related Literature on Hispanic/Latinos, 1990–2001 [electronic resource]

National Cancer Institute, U.S. Dept of Health and Human Services

Internet access: http://purl.access.gpo.gov/GPO/LPS19290

> **HINT:** Many college libraries as well as public libraries are now part of library networks. This network expands the holdings of every library because one library will loan books to another. Therefore, if a book you need is unavailable in your library, ask a librarian about an interlibrary loan. Understand, however, that you may have to wait several days for its delivery. Periodical articles usually come quickly by fax or e-mail transfer.

2c Searching the Library's Electronic Databases

At the computer, search the library's network of electronic databases. You will find a list of these search engines at a link on the library's home page, usually near the electronic book catalog. Each one has a singular mission: to take you directly to articles on your subject, with abstracts in most cases and full text in many others. Thus, you can print or download numerous documents, all relevant to your subject. For example, InfoTrac is a popular database because it covers many subjects. This list gives a few of the sources found by searching on the keyword *coffee*.

> <u>Acrylamide found in coffee</u>. (*ingredients*). (Brief Article)
> *Food Engineering & Ingredients* Dec 2002 v27 i6 p35(1) (88 words)
> <u>Text</u>
>
> <u>The complexity of coffee: One of life's simple pleasures is really quite complex</u> (growth, harvesting, processing, and brewing) Ernesto Illy
> *Scientific American* June 2002 v286 i6 p86(6) (2993 words)
> <u>Text</u>
>
> <u>Muddy waters: The lore, the lure, the lowdown on America's favorite addiction</u> (coffee, coffee madness)
> (Cover story) Mark Schapiro
> *Utne Reader* Nov–Dec 1994 n66 p58(8)
> <u>Abstract</u>

Clicking on an underlined hyperlink accesses the article for your use. As shown above, the third source provides only an abstract, but the first two citations provide the full text of the article, which you can print or download to your files. Remember to save them as text files.

General Databases

In addition to InfoTrac, there are many other general databases that will serve your initial investigation. These databases are sometimes general in order to index many articles on a wide variety of topics. Start with one of these if you have a general keyword for your research but not a specific and focused topic.

BOOKS IN PRINT	This database lists all books currently in print and available from publishers.
CQ RESEARCHER	This collection provides in-depth reports on topics of current interest.

ENCYCLOPEDIA
BRITANNICA | This reference covers all subjects with brief, well-organized articles.

FIRSTSEARCH | This database covers a wide variety of topics and directs you to both articles and books.

GPO | This site for the U.S. Government Printing Office gives you access to all government publications on all subjects.

INFORME! | This database offers an index to articles in Spanish-language magazines.

INGENTA | This site provides general information on a vast variety of topics. However, Ingenta is a commercial site, and you will have to pay for articles you download or order by fax.

NETLIBRARY | This database carries you to books on all subjects, including e-books. To access a book online, you need both a username and a password, which are available from a librarian.

ONLINE BOOKS PAGE | Maintained by the University of Pennsylvania, this site gives you access to books on all subjects, with options for printing and downloading the pages.

OXFORD
REFERENCE ONLINE | This database offers you the full text of 135 reference books published by Oxford University Press. The sources cover all general subjects. See your librarian to secure the username and password necessary for entry into the database.

By investigating two or three of the databases listed above, you should gain a quick start on your initial investigation into a subject. The sources that you download or print will help focus your topic and help frame your thesis sentence.

Databases by Discipline

Your library also houses subject-specific databases. Thus, you can examine a specialized database for articles on health issues or, if you prefer, history, and many others. Listed next, by subject area, are a few databases to help launch your investigation. *Note:* These sources are available only through your library access, and in some cases they require an additional username and password that you must request from your librarian.

Literature

CONTEMPORARY LITERARY CRITICISM	A database that indexes critical articles about contemporary authors. It is thus a good source if you are examining the work of a twenty-first-century writer.
LION	This database provides full-text poems, drama, and fiction. It includes biographies, literary criticism, guides to analysis of literary works, and even video readings by writers.
LITFINDER	This source is a search engine for finding poems, stories, plays, and essays.
MLA BIBLIOGRAPHY	This is a major database for all significant articles of criticism on literature, linguistics, and folklore.

History

AMERICA: HISTORY AND LIFE	This is a first-rate database covering all the important articles in this area.
WORLD HISTORY FULLTEXT	A database to full-text articles in all phases of world history.
VIVA	This database focuses on history with an emphasis on women's studies.

Education, Psychology, and Social Issues

ERIC	This giant database takes you quickly to articles and some books with a focus

primarily on education but with full coverage of social and communication topics.

PROJECTMUSE This database provides current issues of about 200 journals in the fields of education, cultural studies, political science, gender studies, literature, and others. It also links you to JSTOR (see the next entry) for past issues of the journals.

JSTOR The acronym stands for "journal storage" because this database maintains the images of thousands of academic articles in their original form and with original page numbers. It centers on the social sciences but includes articles from other fields, such as literature.

PSYCINFO This database houses a massive index of articles and books in psychology, medicine, education, and social work.

Health, Medicine, Fitness, and Nutrition

CINAHL The initials stand for *Cumulative Index to Nursing and Allied Health Literature*, which is a giant database for sources in nursing, public health, and the allied fields of nutrition and fitness.

HEALTH AND WELLNESS This database indexes a wide array of articles in medicine, nutrition, fitness, and public health.

PUBMED This source indexes articles on dentistry as well as nursing and medicine.

The Arts

GROVE DICTIONARY OF ART This source is an online art encyclopedia, not a database. It contains information from the *Dictionary of Art* and features about 45,000 articles on painting, sculpture, architecture, and other visual arts.

GROVE DICTIONARY
OF MUSIC   Like the one above, this source is an online encyclopedia with 29,000 articles drawn from the printed versions of the *New Grove Dictionary of Music and Musicians*, *New Grove Dictionary of Opera*, and *New Grove Dictionary of Jazz*. It covers the various aspects of music, such as instrumentation, orchestral performance, voice, as so forth.

MUSIC INDEX   This database provides a citation index to 655 journals on a broad range of musical topics, including reviews. However, it is a citation-only database, so no abstracts or full-text are provided. On that subject, however, see the Hint on page 25.

Computers, Business, Technology

GENERAL BUSINESS
FILE   This database provides abstracts and some full-text articles to issues in business, and industry. It includes company profiles and some Wall Street reports.

SAFARI TECH BOOKS
ONLINE   This database focuses on e-commerce and computer science, with information on programming and technology management.

FAITS   The Faulkner Advisory of Information Technology Studies is a database of articles in wireless communications, data networking, security, the Internet, and product comparisons.

The Physical Sciences

AGRICOLA   This database provides an index to articles and book references for agriculture, animal, and plant sciences.

BIOONE   This site provides articles on the biological, ecological, and environmental sciences.

GEOREF   This database carries you to articles in geology and related subjects.

WILEYINTERSCIENCE   This database is loaded with articles on science and biochemistry.

The databases shown above represent just a portion of those available at most college libraries, and more databases are being added monthly. Your task is to determine which databases are available at your library and react accordingly. Obviously, small libraries do not have the same online resources that you will find at the library of a major university. If databases are limited, you may need to consult the printed bibliographies and indexes, as discussed in section 2d.

> ■ **HINT:** If the databases to periodicals shown above provide a citation but not the full text, you can probably retrieve the article in one of two ways: (1) try using the library's electronic book catalog (see section 2b above) to retrieve the journal itself and thereby access the article, or (2) go into the stacks at your library, find the journal, and photocopy the article.

2d   Searching the Printed Bibliographies

A bibliography tells you what books and articles are available on a specific subject. If you have a clearly defined topic, skip to page 26, "Searching in the Specialized Bibliographies and Reference Works." If you are still trying to formulate a clear focus, begin with one of these general guides to titles of books to refine your search.

Searching in General Bibliographies

Some works are broad-based references to books on many subjects:

Bibliographic Index: A Cumulative Bibliography of Bibliographies (in print and online)

Where to Find What: A Handbook to Reference Service

Guide to Reference Books

Figure 2.1 shows how *Bibliographic Index* will send you to bibliographic lists inside books. In this case, the bibliography will be found on pages 105–12 of Sarnoff's book.

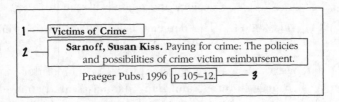

FIGURE 2.1
Example from Bibliographic Index, *2000, shows (1) subject heading, (2) entry of a book that contains a bibliography on crime, (3) specific pages on which the bibliography is located.*

If it fits your research, you would probably want to write a Works Cited entry for this source, as explained on pages 182–185. The MLA citation would look like this:

> Sarnoff, Susan Kiss. <u>Paying for Crime: The Policies and Possibilities of Crime Victim Reimbursement.</u> New York: Praeger, 1996. 105–12.

Searching in the Specialized Bibliographies and Reference Works

After you have narrowed your subject, search one or two of the discipline-specific guides and bibliographies listed below under three categories—humanities, social sciences, sciences. In the main, these are well-indexed references that can take you to more specific books. One of them can help you launch your investigation. Librarians at the reference desk can help you find them, and some are available online.

Humanities	
Art	*Bibliographic Guide to Art and Architecture*
	Fine Arts: A Bibliographic Guide
Drama	*American Drama Criticism: Interpretations*
	Cambridge Guide to Theatre
History	*Dictionary of American History*
	Goldentree Bibliographies in History

Literature	*Dictionary of Literary Biography*
	Essay and General Literature Index
Music	*Music Reference and Research Materials*
	Bibliographic Guide to Music
Philosophy	*Oxford Companion to Philosophy*
	Research Guide to Philosophy
Religion	*Reference Works for Theological Research*
	Who's Who in Religion

Social Sciences

Business	*Bibliographic Guide to Business and Economics*
	Business Information Sources
Education	*Education: A Guide to Reference and Information Sources*
	Resources in Education
Political Science	*International Bibliography of Political Science*
	Political Science: A Bibliographical Guide to the Literature
Psychology	*Annual Reviews of Psychology*
	Psychology: A Guide to Reference and Information Sources
	Bibliographical Guide to Psychology
Sociology	*References Sources in Social Work*
	Sociology: A Guide to Reference and Information Sources
Speech	*Research and Source Guide for Students in Speech Pathology and Audiology*
	Speech Monographs
Women's Studies	*American Women Writers: A Critical Reference Guide*
	Women's Studies Index

Sciences

Astronomy	*The Cambridge Atlas of Astronomy*
	Dictionary of Astronomy
Biology	*Henderson's Dictionary of Biological Terms*
	Information Sources in the Life Sciences

Chemistry	*How to Find Chemical Information: A Guide for Practicing Chemists, Teachers, and Students*
	Lange's Handbook of Chemistry
Computer	*ACM Guide to Computing Literature*
Science	*Bibliographic Guide to the History of Computing, Computers, and the Information Processing Industry*
Health	*Black's Medical Dictionary*
	Cumulated Index Medicus
Physics	*Information Sources in Physics*
	Physics Abstracts

2e Searching the Printed Indexes

An index furnishes the exact page number(s) to articles in magazines, journals, and newspapers. When you have a well-developed idea of your topic, go to the specialized indexes of your discipline, such as *Music Index* or *Philosopher's Index* (either online at your library's computer or in print at the reference section of your library). If labeled an *index*, it may or may not include an abstract. If labeled as an index to abstracts each entry will be an abstract. *Note*: An abstract is a brief description of an article, usually written by the author. An index to abstracts can accelerate your work by allowing you to read the abstract before you assume the task of locating and reading the entire work.

Starting with a General Index to Periodicals

A number of indexes are broad based to list articles in journals from many disciplines. These are good places to begin your research because the indexes have multiple entries and, in some cases, the articles are not so technical and scholarly as those indexed in specialized indexes. For general information on current events, consult *Readers' Guide to Periodical Literature*, which indexes such magazines such as *Aging, Foreign Affairs, Psychology Today, American Scholar, Scientific Review*, and many others. An entry from *Readers' Guide to Periodical Literature* follows:

BRAIN STIMULATION IMPLANTS
Now, electronic 'eyes' for the blind [work of W. H. Dobelle]
O. Port. Il Business Week no3666 p56+ Ja 31 2000

■ **FIGURE 2.2**
From Readers' Guide to Periodical Literature *showing subject, title, author, and publication data.*

Make a bibliography entry for your research journal if it looks promising:

Port, O. "Now, Electronic 'Eyes' for the Blind."
<u>Business Week</u> 31 Jan. 2000: 56+.

Searching Indexes to Topics in the Humanities

Humanities Index (in print or online) catalogs 260 publications in several fields:

archaeology	folklore	performing arts
classical studies	history	philosophy
language and literature	literary	religion
area studies	political criticism	theology

MLA International Bibliography (in print and online) indexes most of the journals in language and literature studies. The printed versions are not kept up to date, so supplement the printed version with the electronic database, if available.

Abstracts of English Studies (in print or online) is an excellent place to begin research in literature studies.

Dissertation Abstracts International—A: Humanities and Social Sciences (in print and online) provides an index to the abstracts of all American dissertations. In the print version, look for issue No. 12, Part 11, of each volume, which contains the cumulated subject and author indexes for issues 1–12 of the volume's two sections.

Searching Indexes to Topics in the Social Sciences

Social Sciences Index (in print and online) indexes journal articles for 263 periodicals in these fields:

anthropology	geography	political
economics	law and criminology	science
environmental	medical science	psychology
science		sociology

Dissertation Abstracts International—A: Humanities and Social Sciences (see above).

Searching Indexes to Topics in the Physical Sciences

Applied Science and Technology Index (in print or online) for articles in chemistry, engineering, computer science, electronics, geology, mathematics, photography, physics, and other related fields.

Biological and Agricultural Index (in print or online) for articles in biology, zoology, botany, agriculture, and related fields.

Dissertation Abstract International—B: Sciences and Engineering (in print or online) provides an index to the abstracts of all American dissertations in the fields of science and engineering. In the print version, look for issue No. 12, Part 11, of each volume, for it contains the cumulated subject and author indexes for issues 1–12 of the volume's two sections.

Searching Indexes to Discipline-Specific Information

In addition to these general indexes, you should examine the indexes for your discipline as listed below in alphabetical order. Some are online by library access; others are found in printed versions in the library's reference room.

Art Index	*Chemical Abstracts*
Biological Abstracts	*Communication Abstracts*
Business Periodicals Index	*Computer Literature Index*
Economic Articles, Index of	*Philosopher's Index*
Education Index	*Physical Education Index*
Engineering Index	*Physics Abstracts*
Environment Abstracts	*Political Science Abstracts,*
Geo Abstracts	*International*
Historical Abstracts	*Psychological Abstracts*
Literature, Cumulative Index	*Religion Index One*
Mathematical Reviews	*Sociological Abstracts*
Music Index	*Women's Studies Index*
Nursing and Allied Health	

2f   Searching Biographies

Biographies of important people appear in books and articles, so you need to use a variety of sources. The electronic book catalog (see section 2b) is a place to start with keywords, such as "biography + index," which lead to links to *Biography Index, Index to Literary Biography,* and many more. Otherwise, use the person's name as a keyword; for example, entering "Ben Franklin" will produce a reference to Cecil B. Currey's biography entitled *Ben Franklin: Patriot or Spy*.

In the library, examine these printed reference books:

Biography Index is a starting point for studies of famous persons. It leads to biographical information for people of all lands.

Current Biography Yearbook provides a biographical sketch of notable people. Most articles are three to four pages in length and, of importance, they include references to other sources at the end. It is current, thorough, and international in scope.

Contemporary Authors provides a biographical guide for current writers in fiction, nonfiction, poetry, journalism, drama, motion pictures, television, and a few other fields. It describes most contemporary writers, giving biographical facts (including a current address and agent), sidelights, and, in many cases, an interview with the author. A bibliography of additional sources is usually included.

Dictionary of Literary Biography profiles thousands of writers in over 100 volumes under such titles as *American Humorists, Victorian Novelists,* or *American Newspaper Journalists*. A comprehensive index helps you locate the article on the author you are researching.

HINT: To find biographical reference works in a specific discipline, such as music or history, consult the library's electronic book catalog with a request such as "biographies of artists." It will then provide hyperlinks to *Who's Who in American Art* and other similar works.

2g   Searching Newspaper Indexes

Newspapers provide contemporary information. At the electronic catalog, ask for a particular newspaper and then use its archival search engine to find articles on your topic. For example, asking for the Nashville *Tennessean* provides the link to the newspaper. Then, entering a keyword such as "state lottery" provides access to articles in the current and previous editions of the *Tennessean*, as shown by this opening to an article:

Lawmaker: Home-schoolers shouldn't have tougher ACT mark
By DUREN CHEEK
Staff Writer
The **state**'s top lawyer was asked yesterday whether Tennessee's **lottery**-funded scholarship program is unconstitutional because it requires home-schooled students to meet higher standards than others entering college.
The request for an opinion came from **state** Rep. Glen Casada, R-College Grove, who said he thinks requiring home-schooled students to score a 23 on their ACT to qualify, while public school students must score only 19, is unfair and discriminatory.
"Proponents of a **lottery** did not mention discriminating against home-schooled students in the **lottery** debate last fall," said Casada, referring to the **lottery** referendum last November. Parents across the **state** were led to believe that students who met a certain criteria would receive a scholarship, period."

■ FIGURE 2.3
Opening paragraphs of an article in The [Nashville] Tennessean.

If your library's electronic catalog cannot access a specific newspaper you want, go to the Internet at *www.newspapers.com*. See pages 47–48 for more information.

In your library, visit also the contemporary reading room, where you will find current issues of local and national newspapers on display for your reading pleasure or for research.

2h Searching the Indexes to Pamphlet Files

Librarians routinely clip items of interest from newspapers, bulletins, pamphlets, and miscellaneous materials and file them alphabetically by subject in loose-leaf folders. Make the pamphlet file a regular stop during preliminary investigation. Sometimes called the *vertical file*, it contains clippings on many topics, such as carpal tunnel syndrome, asbestos in the home, and medical care plans. Two helpful pamphlets, online and in print, are *SIRS* and *CQ Researcher*.

Social Issues Resources Series (SIRS) collects articles on special topics and reprints them as one unit on a special subject, such as abortion, AIDS, prayer in schools, and pollution. With *SIRS*, you get ten or twelve articles readily available in one booklet.

The *CQ Researcher*, like *SIRS*, devotes one pamphlet to one topic, such as "energy and the environment." It will then examine central issues on the topic, give background information, show a chronology of important events or processes, express an outlook, and provide an annotated bibliography.

HINT: For the correct citation forms to articles found in *SIRS* or *CQ Researcher*, see page 225.

2i Searching Government Documents

All branches of the government publish and make available valuable material. At the library's list of available databases, click on GPO, which links you to the files of the Government Printing Office in Washington, DC. Just enter your keywords at the GPO database, such as "SAT Scores," and the search engine will give you links to available documents. You can also search government documents on the Internet by entering *www.GPOAccess.gov* (see "Government," page 42, for additional information). Your library might also house printed copies of these valuable reference tools:

Monthly Catalog of United States Government Publications indexes all the documents published by the Government Printing Office.

Public Affairs Information Service Bulletin (PAIS) indexes articles and documents published by miscellaneous organizations. Its excellent index makes it a good starting point.

Congressional Record provides Senate and House bills, documents, and committee reports.

Public Papers of the Presidents of the United States is the publication of the Executive Branch, including not only the president's papers but also the documents of all members of the president's cabinet and various agencies.

U.S. Code is the publication of the Supreme Court decisions, codes, and other rulings.

HINT: See pages 212–214 for instructions about writing Works Cited entries for government documents.

2j   Searching for Essays within Books

The Essay and General Literature Index (online and in print) helps you find essays hidden within anthologies. It indexes material of both a biographical and a critical nature. The essay listed in the example below might easily have been overlooked by any researcher.

King, Martin Luther, 1929–1968

Raboteau, A. J. Martin Luther King and the tradition of black religious protest. (*In* Religion and the life of the nation; ed. by R. A. Sherrill, p. 46–65).

The library's electronic book catalog will give you the call number for Sherrill's book.

2k   Building Your Research Journal

By now, you should have a collection of printed documents, photocopies, and downloaded files. It's important to keep everything in order with sources clearly marked because you will need to make citations in your text to authors and page numbers, and you will need a Works Cited page that lists full information on each source. These may seem like obvious tasks to you, but reminders are helpful, and we have seen too many instances of students having to abandon perfectly good quotations because they could not find full data on the source for the Works Cited entry.

Build a computer folder. Create a folder on your hard drive for all of your computer files. Carry with you a floppy or zip drive for working at the labs and library. Each time you download an article, you can place it in this folder. As you gather more and more data and begin building an outline, you might create more than one folder.

Name each file precisely. Be descriptive in naming your files so you can identify the content after a few days. A file named *Brown* offers no clue to its contents. Instead, describe the contents—for example, *BrownPesticidesandPets.*

Organize a print folder. You need a notebook with sleeves to keep your written notes, printouts, and photocopies. This too should be organized along the lines of your outline.

Build a rough outline. Early on, write a rough outline to help you organize the mass of material you are gathering. It will also help identify topics needing more research. See page 3 for additional details.

Build a Works Cited file. As you discover sources that fit your outline or sources that you have slotted into your rough draft, enter them in your Works Cited file in alphabetical order. Thus, you accomplish a major task as you work your way through the project. This working bibliography should, at a minimum, contain the author's name, the title of the work, publication information, and a library call number if it's a book you have not yet examined. Shown below is an example, in MLA style, of one student's computer file in progress with three entries.

                    Works Cited
Chivers, Ruth. "Pacific Paradise." <u>Garden Design</u>
    May/June 2005: 64[[endash]]71.
O'Malley, Martin, and John Bowman. "Selling Canada's
    Water." CBS News Online. June 2001. 9 Apr. 2003.
Lichtenthaeler, Gerhard. <u>Political Ecology and the Role
    of Water</u>. Brookfield, VT: Ashgate, 2003.

Your Research Project

1. If you have not done so with an orientation group, take the time to stroll through your library. Identify its various sections and the types of information available there. Especially learn about the reference room, the stacks, and the printed periodical articles. Pick up a bound volume of a journal, open it, and notice how it contains twelve issues (or six) of one year's publications.

2. At the library sit down at one of the computer terminals and investigate its various options. Make up a topic for the moment and go searching for books or articles at the terminal. Try to find an abstract or a full-text article and then print it.

3. Go to the reference desk and ask the librarian for a specialized bibliography on your topic. That is, say something like this, substituting your topic, "Do you have a specialized bibliography on global warming?"

4. Locate the library's holdings of *The CQ Researcher and Social Issues Resources Series*. Page through the various booklets to note how they provide several penetrating articles on a common topic. In the indexes, search to see if your favorite topic has been treated by a special issue.

CHAPTER THREE

SEARCHING
THE WORLD WIDE WEB

Like a library, the Internet is a major source of research information. It makes available millions of computer files relating to any subject—articles, illustrations, sound and video clips, and raw data. However, the Internet cannot replace the library or field research. It offers the best and worst information, and requires careful evaluation. When reading an Internet article, always take time to judge its authority and veracity. This chapter will help you become an efficient searcher for academic information on the Internet.

3a Using a Search Engine

When you know your topic, perform a key search using the words you would like to find in the title, description, or text of an Internet source. For example, to find information on George W. Bush's environmental programs, you would enter the words *George W. Bush* and *environmental programs*. The search engine will direct you to a list of Web sites as shown, for example, by these three hyperlinks: <u>George W. Bush on Environment, George W. Bush's Policies and Plans, The Environmental Legacy of Governor George W. Bush</u>. You can then read the articles to determine if they relate to your research.

Using General Search Engines
About 100 excellent search engines are available. Some of the more popular are listed below. Many sites entice you with advertisements for

various products, but they do an excellent job of directing you to a wide variety of sources. Experiment with them and select the one that works best for you.

Subject Directory Search Engines are compiled by humans and indexed to guide you to general areas that are then subdivided into narrower categories. Your choice of category controls the list.

About.com	**http://home.about.com/index.htm**
Go.network	**http://www.go.com**
Lycos	**http://www.lycos.com**
Yahoo!	**http://www.yahoo.com**

Robot-Driven Search Engines perform a keyword search by electronically scanning millions of Web pages. Your keyword phrase and Boolean operators control the list.

AltaVista	**http://altavista.digital.com**
Excite	**http://www.excite.com**
Google	**http://www.google.com**
Hotbot	**http://www.hotbot.com**
Webcrawler	**http://webcrawler.com**

Find one you prefer, but keep in mind that search engines are designed in different ways. AltaVista, for example, gives you a massive number of results from its more than 22 million Web pages. Yahoo!, on the other hand, is an edited site with directories and subdirectories.

Metasearch Engines simultaneously query about ten major search engines, such as those listed above, and provide you with a short, relevant set of results. You get fewer results than would appear at one of the major search engines. For example, "chocolate+children" produced 342,718 hits on AltaVista but only fifty on Mamma.com. A metasearch engine selects the first few listings from each of the search engines under the theory that each engine puts the most relevant results at the top of its list. This theory may or may not be true. Here are three metasearch engines:

Dogpile	**http://dogpile.com**
. Mamma.com	**http://mamma.com**
Metacrawler.com	**http://metacrawler.com**

CHECKLIST BOOKMARKS

Most Web browser programs, such as Netscape, include a bookmark tool that enables you to save Web addresses for quick access should you wish to revisit the site. For example, in Netscape, simply click on Bookmarks, then click on Add Bookmark. This will automatically add the current URL to the list of bookmarks. In Microsoft Internet Explorer, use the button bar marked Favorites to record an address. Bookmarks can easily be titled and organized so that you could have a bookmark file devoted to a list of sites related to your research paper. *Note:* If you are working at a university computer laboratory, do not add bookmarks to the hard drive. Instead, save the bookmarks to your disk by using Save As in the File menu of Netscape.

3b Using Search Engines Devoted to Academic Disciplines

Many search engines specialize in one area, such as Edweb (education studies) or Envirolink (environmental studies). The following list contains sites that may be helpful in launching your investigation of Internet resources.

Humanities
Art

Art Resource **http://www.artres.com/c/htm/Home.aspx** This site features the world's largest stock photo archive with a keyword-searchable index.

World Wide Arts Resources **http://wwar.world-arts-resources.com** This site provides an artist index as well as an index to exhibits, festivals, meetings, and performances. Its search engine will take you to fine arts departments, online courses, syllabi, and art institutions.

History

Archiving Early America **http://earlyamerica.com** This site displays eighteenth-century documents in their original form for reading and downloading, such as the Bill of Rights and the speeches of Washington, Paine, Jefferson, and others.

Humanities Hub **http://www.gu.edu.au/gwis/hub.hom.html** This site provides resources in the humanities and social sciences with links to anthropology, architecture, cultural studies, film, gender studies, government, history, philosophy, sociology, and women.

Literature

EServer **http://eserver.org** This site provides academic resources in the humanities, including drama, fiction, film, television, and history.

Open Directory Project **http://dmoz.org/Arts/Literature/** This site provides a directory, with links, to specific pieces of literature.

Voice of the Shuttle **http://vos.ucsb.edu** For the literary scholar, this site gives a massive collection of bibliographies, textual criticism, newsgroups, and links to classical studies, history, philosophy, and other related disciplines.

Philosophy

The American Philosophical Association **http://www.apa.udel.edu/apa/** This site provides articles, bibliographies, software, a bulletin board, gopher server, and links to other philosophy sites containing college courses, journals, texts, and newsletters.

Episteme Links: Philosophy Resources on the Internet **http://www.epistemelinks.com/** This site offers links to biographies, philosophical movements, and full-text works.

> **HINT:** If you have problems accessing a particular site, try truncating the address by cutting items from the end. For example, cut **http://www.emory.edu/WHSC/medweb.medlibs.html** to **http://www.emory.edu.** At this main page of the Web site, you can search for whatever file you need.

Religion

Comparative Religion **http://www.comparative-religion.com** This comprehensive site gives references and resources to all religions and religious studies and religious organizations.

Vanderbilt Divinity School **http://www.library.vanderbilt.edu/ divinity/index.html** This source gives references to and interpretations of the Bible, links to other religious Web sites, and online journals, such as *Biblical Archaeologist.*

Social Sciences
Business

All Business Network **http://www.all-biz.com** This site provides a search engine to businesses with relevant information for the following—newsletters, organizations, newsgroups, and magazines.

Finance: The World Wide Web Virtual Library **http://fisher.oso.edu/ fin/overview.html** The Finance Department of Ohio State University has established a site that will link you to hundreds of articles and resource materials on banks, insurers, market news, jobs, and miscellaneous data for students.

Communication

Communication Resources on the Web **http://communication. utsa.edu/commresources.html** This large database takes you to resources and Web sites on associations, book reviews, bibliographies, libraries, media, information science programs, and departments of communication in various universities.

Education

Educom **http://www.educom.com** This site has full-text online articles with a focus on educational technology in its *Educom Review,* a focus on information technology in *Edupage,* and general news from *Educom Update.*

Edweb **http://www.edwebproject.org/resource.cntnts.html** This site focuses on educational issues and resource materials for grades K–12 with articles on Web education, history, and resources.

ERIC (Educational Resource and Information Center) **http://www. eric.ed.gov** ERIC is considered the primary source of research information for most educators. It contains about 1 million documents, available by keyword search, on all aspects of teaching and learning, lesson plans, administration, bibliographies, and almost any topic related to the classroom.

Government

Fedworld **http:// www.fedworld.gov** This site gives you links to Web sites of government departments as well as lists of free catalogs. It links you to the Internal Revenue Service and other government agencies.

Library of Congress **http://www.lcweb.loc.gov** This site provides the Library of Congress catalog online for books by author, subject, and title. It also links to historical collections and research tools, such as Thomas, where you have access to congressional legislation.

White House Web **http://www.whitehouse.gov** This site provides a graphical tour, messages from the President and the Vice President, and accounts of life at the White House. Visitors to this site can even leave a message for the President in the guest book.

Political Science

Political Science Resources on the Web **http://www.lib.umich.edu/ govdocs.poliscinew.html** This site at the University of Michigan is a vast data file on government information—local, state, federal, foreign, and international. It is a good site for political theory and international relations, with links to dissertations, periodicals, reference sources, university courses, and other social science information.

Psychology

Encyclopedia of Psychology **http://www.psychology.org/links/ Resources/Doing_Research/** This site features a collection of articles for preparing psychology documents from research with current and archival information.

PsycINFO **http://www.apa.org/psycinfo/** The American Psychological Association (APA) maintains this excellent site for current and archival information in the various disciplines.

Sociology

Social Science Information Gateway (SOSIG) **http://sosig.ac.uk** The SOSIG site allows a keyword search that makes available to you many Web sites in an alphabetical list.

Sociology **http://hakatai.mcli.dist.maricopa.edu/smc/ml/sociology. html** This site gives you access to hundreds of sites that provide articles and resource materials on almost all aspects of sociology issues.

Women's Studies

The Women's Resource Project **http://www.ibiblio.org/cheryb/ women/** This site links you to libraries on the Web that have collections on women's studies. It also has links to women's programs and women's resources on the Web.

Women's Studies Database **http://www.mith2.umd.edu/ womensstudies/** This site features a search engine for a keyword search of women's issues and provides directories to bibliographies, classic texts, references, course syllabi from various universities, and gateways to several other Web sites.

Sciences
Astronomy

American Astronomical Society **http://www.aas.org** This site features the *Astrophysical Journal*, which provides articles, reviews, and educational information. The site also links to other astronomy Web sites.

Science at NASA **http://science.nasa.gov/Astronomy.htm** This site links you to NASA programs, such as the space station, the shuttle program, or Project Galileo. It provides maps of the planets, views of Earth from many different angles, and plenty of planetary information.

Computer and Internet Technology

Computer Science **http://library.albany.edu/subject/csci.htm** This site is a good starting point for students because it provides numerous links to resources in the computer disciplines.

Internet Society (ISOC) **http://www.isoc.org** This site is supported by the companies, agencies, and foundations that launched the Internet and that keep it functioning. It gives vital information through articles from the *ISOC Forum* newsletter.

Virtual Computer Library **http://www.utexas.edu/computer/ucl** This site gives access to academic computing centers at the major universities along with books, articles, and bibliographies.

Environmental Science

Envirolink **http://envirolink.org** This site has a search engine that allows access to environmental articles, photographs, action alerts, organizations, and additional Web sources.

The Virtual Library of Natural Science and Mathematics **http://vlib.org/Science** This site provides valuable links to other Web sites in categories such as endangered species, global sustainability, and pollution.

General Science

The Academy of Natural Sciences **http://www.acnatsci.org/library/index.html** This site will link you to hundreds of articles and resource materials on various issues and topics in the natural sciences.

BIOSIS **http://www.biosis.org/** This site provides searchable databases in biology and life sciences and serves as an excellent resource for students wishing to conduct scientific research.

National Academy of Sciences **http://www.nas.edu** This comprehensive site combines the resources of the National Academy of Engineering, the Institute of Medicine, and the National Research Council. It focuses on math and science education and offers links to scientific societies.

Health and Medicine

Global Health **http://www.globalhealth.gov** This Web page provides articles on environmental destruction, overpopulation, infectious diseases, the consequences of war, and, in general, the health of the globe. It offers links to other journals, newsletters, and government documents that explore environmental issues.

Medweb: Medical Libraries **http://www.medweb.emory.edu/medweb/** Emory University provides a site that connects with medical libraries and their storehouses of information. It also gives links to other health-related Web sites.

National Institutes of Health **http://www.nih.gov** NIH leads the nation in medical research, so this site provides substantive information on numerous topics, from cancer and diabetes to malpractice and medical ethics. It provides links to online journals for the most recent news in medical science.

> ■ **HINT:** You can quickly build a bibliography on the Internet in two ways: (1) At a search engine such as AltaVista, enter a descriptive phrase such as *child abuse bibliographies*, and (2) Use the search engines of Amazon **www.amazon.com** and Barnes and Noble **www.bn.com** to gather a list of books currently in print. Then, find the books at your library.

3c Accessing Online Sources

Several types of sources are available, and you should use more than one type in your research.

Internet Home Pages

You can locate home pages for individuals, institutions, and organizations by using a search engine such as Yahoo! and AltaVista (see page 38). Type in a person's name or the name of an organization, such as the American poet James Dickey, and you will get a link to the site **http://www.jamesdickey.org/DickeyNFPoet.html.** The home page will provide links, a directory, an index, and an internal search engine that will take you quickly to specific material.

Internet Articles on the Web

A search engine will direct you to many articles on the Web, some isolated without documentation and credentials and others that list the author as well as the association to which the author belongs. For example, a search for *child care centers* will produce local sites such as Apple Tree Family Child Care. Private sites like these will infuse local knowledge into your research. Adding another relevant term, such as *child care regulations*, will take you to state and national sites such as the National Resource Center for Health and Safety in Child Care.

HINT: An Internet article that contains only a title and the URL cannot be properly documented and should be avoided.

Journal Articles on the Web

The Internet supplies journal articles of two types: (1) articles in online journals designed and published only on the Web, and (2) reproductions of articles that have appeared in printed journals. Find them in three ways.

- Using your favorite search engine, enter a keyword phrase for journals plus the name of your subject. For example, one student, using AltaVista, entered a keyword search for *journals+fitness* and found links to twenty journals devoted to fitness, including *Health Page*, *Excite Health*, and *Physical Education*.

- Access a search engine's subject directory. In Yahoo!, for example, one student selected Social Science from the key directory, clicked on Sociology, clicked on Journals, and accessed links to several online journals, such as *Sociological Research Online* and *Edge: The E-Journal of Intercultural Relations*.

- If you already know the name of a journal, go to your favorite search engine to make a keyword query such as *Psycholoquy*, a social science journal.

Note: Some journals furnish an abstract but require a fee for access to the full text.

HINT: Remember that abstracts may not accurately represent the full article. In fact, some abstracts are not written by the author at all but by an editorial staff. Resist the desire to copy quotations from the abstract; instead, write a paraphrase or, better, find the full text and cite from it.

Magazine Articles on the Web

The Internet supplies magazine articles of two types. Some appear in original online magazines designed and published only on the Web.

Others are reproductions of articles that have appeared in printed magazines. Several directories exist for finding magazine articles:

> NewsDirectory.com **http://www.newsdirectory.com** This site takes you to magazine home pages, where you can begin your search in that magazine's archives. A search for *current events*, for example, will send you to *Atlantic Monthly* **theatlantic.com**, *Harper's* **harpers.org**, or *Newsweek* **Newsweek.com.**
>
> Electric Library **http://www.highbeam.com/library/index.asp** This Web site has a subscription-based search engine with links to 17 million documents in newspapers, magazines, and news services. You can get free access for seven days. Remember to cancel your membership after finishing your research or charges will accrue.
>
> Pathfinder **http://pathfinder.com/** This site gives free access to *Time* magazine and has a good search engine with links to thousands of archival articles.
>
> ZD Net **http://www.zdnet.com/** This site provides excellent access to industry-oriented articles on banking, electronics, computers, and management. You can receive two weeks of free access before charges begin to accrue.

You can also access online magazines through a search engine's directory. For example, using AltaVista, one student clicked on Health and Fitness in the subject directory of the home page, clicked next on Publications and then Magazines. The result was a list of forty magazines devoted to various aspects of health and fitness, such as *Healthology* and *The Black Health Net.*

News Sources

Most major news organizations maintain Internet sites. Consult one of these:

> CNN Interactive **http://www.cnn.com** This search engine takes you quickly, without cost, to transcripts of CNN broadcasts, making it a good source for research in current events.

C-SPAN Online **http://www.c-span.org** This site emphasizes public affairs and offers both a directory and a search engine with links to transcripts. It is a valuable source for research in public affairs, government, and political science.

CQ Electronic Library **http://library.cqpress.com/index.php** This Web page keeps tabs on congressional activities in Washington.

National Public Radio Online **http://www.npr.org** This site provides audio articles via RealPlayer or some other audio engine. Be prepared to take careful notes.

The *New York Times* on the Web **http://www.nytimes.com** You can read recent articles for free. However, if you search the 365-day archive, have your credit card ready. Articles cost $2.50. After purchase, they appear on the monitor for printing or downloading.

USA Today DeskTopNews **http://www.usatoday.com** This site's rapid search engine provides information about current events.

U.S. News Online **http://www.usnews.com** This site has a fast search engine and provides free, in-depth articles on current political and social issues.

The *Washington Times* **http://www.washingtontimes.com/** This site is a good source of up-to-the-minute political news.

To find additional newspapers, search for *newspapers* on Yahoo! or AltaVista. Your college library may also provide Lexis-Nexis, which will search online news sources for you.

> **HINT:** Document Internet sources to avoid the appearance of citing from the printed version. Major differences often exist between the same article in *USA Today* and in *USA Today* DeskTopNews.

Books on the Web

One of the best sources of full-text, online books is the Online Books Page at the University of Pennsylvania: **http://digital.library.upenn.edu/books/**. This site indexes books by author, title, and subject. Its search engine takes you quickly to the full text of Thomas Hardy's *A Pair of Blue Eyes* or Linnea Hendrickson's *Children's Literature: A*

Guide to the Criticism. This site adds new textual material almost every day, so consult it first. Understand, however, that contemporary books, still under copyright protection, are not included. That is, you can freely download an Oscar Wilde novel but not one by contemporary writer J. K. Rowling. Here are a few additional sites:

Bartleby.com	**http://www.bartleby.com**
Internet Classics Archive	**http://classics.mit.edu**
Project Gutenberg	**http://promo.net/pg/**
Bibliomania	**http://www.bibliomania.com**
Education Planet	**http://educationplanet.com**
American Literary Classics	**http://www.americanliterature.com**

There are many more; in a search engine, use a keyword request for *full-text books.*

E-mail Discussion Groups

Discussion groups correspond by e-mail on a central topic. For example, your literature professor might ask everybody in the class to join an e-mail discussion group on Victorian literature. To participate, you must have an e-mail address and subscribe to the list. In an online class using Blackboard, for instance, special forums can be designated that request the response of all members in the class. Your participation may contribute to your final grade.

Real-time chatting is also available through immediate messages on the Internet or with members of chat groups. However, we discourage the use of chat commentary for your research. Even though Yahoo!, AltaVista, AOL, and other servers offer access to chat groups, you cannot quote people with fictional usernames and no credentials.

Archives

In addition to searching the archives via your library's electronic catalog (see pages 17–19), you can find documents on the Internet.

1. For archival research in government documents, see Library of Congress **http://www.loc.gov**. This site allows you to search by word, phrase, name, title, series, and number. It provides special features such as an American Memory Home Page, full-text legislative information, and exhibitions such as the drafts of Lincoln's Gettysburg Address.

2. Go to an edited search engine such as Yahoo! to find results quickly. For example, requesting *Native American literature+archives* produced such links as American native press archives, Native American History Archive, Native Americans and the Environment, Indigenous Peoples' Literature, and Sayings of Chief Joseph.

3. Go to a metasearch engine such as **dogpile.com** and make a request such as *Native American literature+archives*. The engine will list such sites as Reference Works and Research Material for Native American Studies **http://www.stanford.edu**. There you would find archives entitled Native American Studies Encyclopedias and Handbooks, Native American Studies Bibliographies, Native American Studies Periodical Indexes, and Native American Biography Resources.

4. Use the directory and subdirectories of a search engine to move deeper and deeper into the files. Remember, this tracing goes quickly. Here is an example that shows how the directories can carry you rather swiftly from a browser's main page to archives of ancient warfare: AltaVista: Society > History > By Time Period > Ancient > Warfare in the Ancient World > The Legend of the Trojan War.

CHECKLIST EVALUATING INTERNET SOURCES

- Prefer the .edu and .org sites. Usually these are domains developed by an educational institution, such as Ohio State University, or by a professional organization, such as the American Psychological Association. The .gov (government) and .mil (military) sites usually have reliable materials.

- The .com (commercial) sites become suspect for several reasons: (1) They sell advertising space, (2) They often charge for access to their files, and (3) They can be ISP (Internet Service Providers) sites where people pay to post material that has not been edited and subjected to peer review.

- What is the date? References in the sciences demand a date because research grows old quickly. For the same reason, look for the date when the Web information was last revised.

- Look for the professional affiliation of the writer, which you will find in the opening credits or an e-mail address. Ask this question: Is the writer affiliated with a professional organization? Information should be included in the opening credit. An e-mail address might also show academic affiliation. Is contact information for the author or sponsoring organization included in the document? Other ways to investigate the credibility of a writer are searching for the writer's home page and looking on Amazon.com for a list of his or her books.

- Can you identify the target audience? What does it tell you about the purpose of the Web site? Remember, the Web sites needed for your research should appeal to the intellectual person.

- What bias colors the Web site? *Note:* There is always a bias of some sort because even academic sites will show bias toward, for example, the grandeur of Greek philosophy, the brilliance of the Allied Forces in World War II, or the artistry of Picasso's Blue period.

- Look at the end of Internet articles for a bibliography of sources which will indicate the scholarly nature of the writer's work.

- Treat e-mail as mail, not as a scholarly source. Academic discussion groups may sometimes contain valuable information, but use it only if you know the source.

- Do not cite from chat forums where fictitious usernames are common.

- Hypertext links to educational sites serve as an academic bibliography to reliable sources. However, if the site gives hypertext links to commercial sites or if spam floods the screen, abandon the site and do not quote from it.

- Learn to distinguish among the different types of Web sites such as advocacy pages, personal home pages, informational pages, and business and marketing pages. One site provides several evaluation techniques that might prove helpful: **http://www.uric.edu/cit/ guides/irg=49.html**.

- Your skills in critical reading and thinking can usually determine the validity of a site. For more information on critical reading, visit this site: **http://www.library.ucla.edu/libraries/college/ help/critical/**.

Your Research Project

1. To look for an Internet discussion group on your topic, go to metacrawler; however, before entering your subject, select the button for searching newsgroups rather than the Web. Explore the choices.

2. Voice of the Shuttle is a large and powerful search engine for educational information. Enter this URL, **http://vos.ucsb.edu/**, and search for your topic. If unsuccessful, try one of the other educational search engines listed on page 40.

3. When you have found an Internet article directly devoted to your subject, apply to it an evaluation checklist as described on pages 50–51. Ask yourself, "Does this site have merit?" Apply that same test to other Internet articles as you find them.

4. Practice using the Bookmark feature of your browser. That is, rather than print an article from the Internet, bookmark it instead for future reference (see page 39).

5. As with library sources, begin making bibliography entries and writing notes of promising Internet sources. Begin building a computer file of promising sources, develop a folder of printouts from the Internet, and save pertinent information that you will need for your Works Cited entries later in the research process (see pages 183–185 for more information on creating a Works Cited page).

CHAPTER FOUR

FIELD RESEARCH: COLLECTING DATA OUTSIDE THE LIBRARY

The human species is distinguished by its ability to examine the world systematically and create pioneers for the millennium, such as computer technicians, microsurgeons, and nuclear engineers. You may become one of them. Each discipline has different expectations in its methods of inquiry and presentation. This chapter introduces you to the variety of field research and the results you might expect.

4a Conducting Research within a Discipline

Some disciplines, more than others, require you to work in the laboratory or the field, not just the library. Attitudes and methods differ among the social, physical, and applied sciences, and those three differ in many ways from the attitudes and methods of humanists.

The Social Scientists

Social scientists work from the assumption that behavior can be observed, tested, and catalogued by observation and experimental testing. Professionals perform thousands of experiments every month. They research stress in the workplace, study the effects of birth order on the youngest child, and develop testing mechanisms, such as the Scholastic Aptitude Test (SAT). As a student in the social sciences, you are asked to perform similar but less exhaustive studies, such as the typing mannerisms of students composing on a computer. If your topic examines any aspect of human behavior (for example, road rage on campus streets), prepare to go into the field for some aspects of your research.

The Physical Scientists

Physical scientists wish to discover, define, and explain the natural world. They operate under the assumption that we can know precise data on flora and fauna, geological formations, the various species of animals, and so forth. You may be asked to join a field expedition to catalog one type of fern, to test the water conditions at a local lake, or to locate sinkholes in a confined area. Laboratory experimentation is also a regular activity of scientists, so any experiments you conduct should be recorded in a lab notebook and may become significant to your written reports. If your topic examines the natural world in some way—for example, the growing deer population in the Governor Oaks subdivision—field research may be useful.

The Applied Scientists

Applied scientists *apply* scientific knowledge to make life more efficient, enduring, and comfortable. By means of mathematical formulas and cutting-edge technology, they launch spaceships to encircle the globe, find new ways to repair broken bones, and discover better methods of movie animation. You, too, can participate in such experiments by designing access facilities for students with wheelchairs (for example, should doors open out or open in?), investigating systems to measure the force of lightning strikes, or examining ways to increase the weight of beef cattle. It is not unusual today for undergraduate students to apply their computer knowledge to the creation of new programs, even new software and hardware. If your research involves application of scientific information, researching in the field may help you formulate your ideas.

The Humanists

Humanists in the fine arts, literature, history, religion, and philosophy have a distinctive approach to knowledge. While scientists usually investigate a small piece of data and its meaning, humanists examine an entire work of art (Verdi's opera *Rigoletto*), a period of history (the Great Depression), or a philosophical theory (existentialism). Humanists usually accept a poem or painting as a valid entity and search it subjectively for what it means to human experience. However, that does not preclude humanists from conducting field research. For example, a student might go to England to retrace the route of late medieval pilgrims to Canterbury, as such a trip might shed new light on Chaucer's poetry. In another instance, a student's field trip to Jackson, Mississippi, might enlighten the scholar on the fiction of Eudora Welty. Conducting archival research on manuscript materials could take you into unknown territory. Your work with a writer living in your locality may prompt you to seek a personal interview, and correspondence with writers and historians is standard fare in humanist research. Thus, if your research in history, religion, or the arts offers the opportunity for field research, add it to your research program.

4b Investigating Local Sources

Interviewing Knowledgeable People

Talk to persons who have experience with your subject. Personal interviews can elicit valuable in-depth information. They provide information that few others will have. Look to organizations for experienced persons. For example, a student writing on a folklore topic might contact the county historian, a senior citizens organization, or a local historical society. If necessary, the student could post a notice soliciting help: "I am writing a study of local folklore. Wanted: People who have a knowledge of regional tales." Another way to accomplish this task is to request information from an e-mail discussion group, which will bring responses from several persons (see pages 5 and 49 for details).

Follow a few general guidelines. Set up your appointments in advance. Consult with persons knowledgeable about your topic. If possible, talk to several people to get a fair assessment. A telephone interview is acceptable, as is e-mail correspondence. Be courteous and on time for interviews. Be prepared with a set of focused, relevant questions. For accuracy and if permitted by the person being interviewed, record the session on audiotape or videotape. Double-check direct quotations with the interviewee or the tape. Get permission before citing a person by name or quoting the person's exact words. Handle private and public papers with great care, and send participants a copy of your report along with a thank-you note. Make a bibliography entry just as you would for a book:

    Thornbright, Mattie Sue. Personal interview. 15 Jan.
      2006.

Writing Letters and Corresponding by E-mail

Correspondence provides a written record for research. Write a letter asking pointed questions that will elicit relevant responses. Tell the person who you are, what you are attempting to do, and why you are writing to him or her.

```
Gena Messersmith
12 Morningside Road
Clarksville, TN
Ms. Rachel G. Warren, Principal
Sango High School
Clarksville, TN

Dear Ms. Warren:
I am a college student conducting research into meth-
ods for handling hyperactive children in the public
school setting. I am surveying each elementary school
principal in the county. I have contacted the cen-
tral office also, but I wished to have perspectives
from those of you on the front lines. I have a child
with ADHD, so I have a personal as well as a schol-
arly reason for this research. I could ask specific
questions on policy, but I have gotten that from
the central office. What I would like from you is
a brief paragraph that describes your policy and pro-
cedure when one of your teachers reports a hyper-
active child. In particular, do you endorse the use
of medication for calming the child with ADHD? May
I quote you in my report? I will honor any request
to withhold your name.
     I have enclosed a self-addressed, stamped enve-
lope for your convenience. You may e-mail me at
messersmithg@apsu.edu.
     Sincerely,
     Gena Messersmith
```

This letter makes a fairly specific request for a minimum amount of information. It does not require an expansive reply. If Gena Messersmith uses a quotation from the reply and if she has permission from the interviewee, she can provide a bibliography entry on her Works Cited page.

```
Warren, Rachel G. Principal of Sango High School,
    Clarksville, TN. E-mail to the author.
    5 Apr. 2004.
```

If Messersmith decides to build a table or graph from replies received, she must document the survey as shown on page 60.

Reading Personal Papers

Search for letters, diaries, manuscripts, family histories, and other personal materials that might contribute to your study. The city library may house private collections, and the public librarian might help you contact the county historian and other private citizens who have important documents. Obviously, handling private papers must be done with the utmost decorum and care. Make a bibliography entry for such materials.

```
Joplin, Lester. "Notes on Robert Penn Warren."
    Unpublished paper. Nashville, 2003.
```

Attending Lectures and Public Addresses

Watch bulletin boards and the newspaper for a public speaker who may contribute to your research. At the lecture, take careful notes, and if the speaker makes one available, secure a copy of the lecture or speech. If you want to use your equipment to make an audiotape or videotape of a speech, courtesy demands that you seek permission. Remember, too, that many lectures, reproduced on video, are available in the library or in departmental files. Always make a bibliography entry for any words or ideas you use.

```
Petty-Rathbone, Virginia. "Edgar Allan Poe and the
    Image of Ulalume." Lecture. Heard Library,
    Vanderbilt U., 2000.
```

Investigating Government Documents

Documents are available at four levels of government: city, county, state, and federal. As a constituent, you are entitled to examine a wide assortment of records on file at various agencies. If your topic demands it, you may contact the mayor's office, attend and take notes at a meeting of the county commissioners, or search for documents in the archives of the state or federal government.

City and County Government Visit the courthouse or county clerk's office to find facts on elections, marriages, births, and deaths as well as census data. These archives include wills, tax rolls, military assignments, deeds to property, and much more. A trip to the local courthouse can help you trace the history of the land and its people.

State Government Contact a state office that relates to your research, such as Consumer Affairs (which provides general information), Public Service Commission (which regulates public utilities such as the telephone company), or the Department of Human Services (which administers social and welfare services). The names of these agencies may vary from state to state. Each state has an archival storehouse and makes its records available for public review.

Federal Government Your United States senator or representative can send you booklets printed by the Government Printing Office (GPO). A list of these materials, many of which are free, appears on the GPO Web site **www.GPOAccess.gov**. In addition, you can gain access to the National Archives Building in Washington, DC, or to one of the regional branches in Atlanta, Boston, Chicago, Denver, Fort Worth, Kansas City, Los Angeles, New York, Philadelphia, or Seattle. Their archives contain court records and government documents that you can review in two books: *Guide to the National Archives of the United States* and *Select List of Publications of the National Archives and Record Service.* You can view some documents on microfilm if you consult the *Catalog of National Archives Microfilm Publications.*

4c Examining Audiovisual Materials, the Internet, and Television

Important data can be found in audiovisual materials. You can find these both on and off campus. Consult such guides as *Educators Guide* (film, film strips, and tapes), *Media Review Digest* (nonprint materials), *Video Source Book* (video catalog), *The Film File*, or *International Index to Recorded Poetry.* Television, with its many channels, such as The History Channel, offers invaluable data. With a VCR, you can record a program for detailed examination. The Internet houses articles on almost every conceivable topic. As for other sources, write bibliography entries for any materials that have merit and contribute to your paper.

> "Nutrition and AIDS." Narr. Carolyn O'Neil. CNN.
> 12 Jan. 1997.

When using media sources, watch closely the opening and closing credits to capture the necessary data for your bibliography entry. The format is explained on page 237. As with the personal interview, be scrupulously accurate in taking notes. Citations may refer to a performer, director, or narrator, depending on the focus of your study. It is best to write direct quotations because paraphrases of television commentary can unintentionally be distorted by bias. Always scrutinize material taken from an Internet site (see pages 50–51 for a checklist of ways to evaluate Internet articles).

4d Conducting a Survey with a Questionnaire

Questionnaires can produce current, firsthand data that you can tabulate and analyze. To achieve meaningful results, you must survey randomly with regard to age, sex, race, education, income, residence, and other factors. Bias can creep into the questionnaire unless you remain objective. Use a formal survey only if you are experienced with tests and measurements and statistical analysis or when you have an instructor who will help you with the instrument. Be advised that most schools have a Human Subjects Committee that sets guidelines, draws up consent forms, and requires anonymity of participants for information-gathering that might be intrusive. An informal survey gathered in the hallways of campus buildings lacks credibility in the research paper. When using media sources, watch closely the opening and closing credits to capture the necessary data for your Works Cited entry. The format is explained on pages 182–185.

Surveys usually depend on *quantitative* methodologies, which produce numerical data. That is, the questionnaire results are tallied to reflect campus crime rates, parking slots for students, or the shifts in student population in off-campus housing. In some cases a survey depends on *qualitative* methodologies; these assess answers to questions on social issues, such as the number of biased words in a history text, the reasons for marijuana use, or levels of hyperactivity in a test group of children.

Label your survey in the bibliography entry:

```
Mason, Valerie, and Sarah Mossman. "Child Care
    Arrangements of Parents Who Attend College."
    Questionnaire. Knoxville: U of Tennessee,
    2004.
```

Keep the questionnaire short, clear, and focused on your topic. Questions must be unbiased. Ask your professor to review the instrument before using it. Design your questionnaire for a quick response to a scale ("Choose A, B, or C"), a ranking (first choice, second choice, and so on), or fill-in blanks. You should also arrange for an easy return of the questionnaire by providing a self-addressed stamped envelope or by allowing respondents to send in their completed questionnaires by e-mail.

Tabulate the responses objectively. Present the results—positive or negative—as well as a sample questionnaire in the appendix to your paper. While results that deny your hypothesis may not support the outcome you desire, they still have value.

4e Conducting Experiments, Tests, and Observation

Empirical research, performed in a laboratory or in the field, can determine why and how things exist, function, or interact with one another. Your paper will explain your methods and findings in pursuit of a hypothesis or theory. An experiment thereby becomes primary evidence for your paper.

Observation occurs generally in the field, which might be a child care center, a movie theater, a parking lot, or the counter of a McDonald's restaurant. The field is anywhere you can observe, count, and record behavior, patterns, and systems. It can be testing the water in a stream or observing the nesting patterns of deer. Retail merchandisers conduct studies to observe buying habits. A basketball coach might gather and analyze data on shot selections by members of his team. Gathering data is a way of life for television executives, politicians, and thousands of marketing professionals.

A *case study* is a formal report based on your observation of a human subject. For example, it might require you to examine patterns of behavior to build a profile. It can be based on biographical data, interviews, tests, and observation. You might observe and interview an older person with dementia; that would be a case study and evidence for your research paper. Each discipline has its own standards for properly conducting a case study. You should not examine any subject without the guidance and approval of your instructor.

Most experiments and observations begin with a *hypothesis*, which is similar to a thesis sentence (see pages 8–11). The hypothesis is a statement assumed to be true for the purpose of investigation. *Hummingbirds live as extended families governed by a patriarch* is a hypothesis for which data are needed to prove its validity. *The majority of people will not correct the poor grammar of a speaker* is a hypothesis for which testing and observation must be conducted to prove its validity.

You can begin observation without a hypothesis and let the results lead you to the implications. Shown below is one student's double-entry format used to record observation on the left and commentary on the right. This is a limited example of field notes.

Record:	Response:
Day 1	
10-minute session at window, 3 hummingbirds fighting over the feeder	Is the male chasing away the female, or is the female the aggressor?
Day 2	
10-minute session at window, saw 8 single hummingbirds at feeder #1 and 1 guarding feeder #2 by chasing others away.	I did some research, and the red-throated male is the one that's aggressive.

Generally, a report on an experiment or observation follows a format that provides four distinct parts: introduction, method, results, and discussion. These four divisions of the scientific report are discussed fully in section 5a, page 69.

CHECKLIST CONDUCTING AN EXPERIMENT
OR OBSERVATION

- Express clearly your hypothesis in the introduction.
- Provide a review of the literature if necessary for establishing an academic background for the work.
- Explain your design for the study—lab experiment, observation, or the collection of raw data in the field.
- Design the work for maximum respect to your subjects. In that regard, you may find it necessary to get approval for your research from a governing board.
- For the results section, maintain careful records and accurate data. Don't let your expectations influence the results.
- Be prepared in your conclusion to discuss your findings and any implications to be drawn.

Your Research Project

1. Look carefully at your subject to determine if research outside the library will be helpful for your project. If so, what kind of research? Correspondence? local records? the news media? a questionnaire? an observation or experiment?

2. Work closely with your instructor to design an instrument that will affect your research and your findings. In fact, most instructors will want to examine any questionnaire that you will submit to others and will want to approve the design of your experiment or observation.

3. For any experiment or investigation with humans or animals, follow university guidelines on testing.

CHAPTER FIVE

ORGANIZING IDEAS
AND SETTING GOALS

Initially, research is haphazard, and your workspace will be cluttered with bits of information on notes and photocopied sheets. After investigating and gathering sufficient sources for your project, you need to organize the information to serve specific needs. The structure of your project will become clear only when you organize your research materials into a proposal, a list of ideas, a set of questions, or a rough outline. In most cases, the design of your study should match an appropriate organizational model, sometimes called a *paradigm*, which means "an example that serves as a pattern or model." The organizational models in this chapter will help you organize your notes, photocopies, and downloaded files. After all, each scholarly field gives a special insight into any given topic, and each research assignment will demand its own approaches that produce different kinds of papers in a variety of formats for the discipline involved. By following an academic model, you can be assured that your research project will have the correct design to meet the demands of the assignment.

5a Using the Correct Academic Model (Paradigm)

A traditional outline, because it is content-specific, is useful for one paper only, while an academic pattern, like those shown below, governs all papers within a certain design. For example, a general, all-purpose model gives a plan for almost any research topic.

A General, All-Purpose Model

If you are uncertain about your assignment, start with this basic model and expand it with your own material to develop a detailed outline. Readers, including your instructor, are accustomed to this sequence for research papers. It offers plenty of leeway.

- Identify the subject in the *introduction.* Explain the problem, provide background information, and give a clear thesis statement.
- Analyze the subject in the *body* of the paper. You can compare, analyze, give evidence, trace historical events, and handle other matters.
- Discuss your findings in the *conclusion.* You can challenge an assumption, interpret the findings, provide solutions, or reaffirm your thesis.

The specific design of any model is based on the nature of the assignment and the discipline for which you are writing. Each of the following forms is explained below.

Academic Pattern for the Interpretation of Literature and Other Creative Works

If you plan to interpret a musical, artistic, or literary work, such as an opera, a group of paintings, or a novel, adjust this next model to your subject and purpose and build it, with your factual data, into a working outline.

Introduction

Identify the work.

Give a brief summary in one sentence.

Provide background information that relates to the thesis.

Offer biographical facts about the artist that relate to the specific issues.

Quote and paraphrase authorities to establish the scholarly traditions.

Write a thesis sentence that establishes your particular views of the literary work.

Body

Provide evaluative analysis divided by imagery, theme, design, use of color, character development, structure, symbolism, narration, language, musical themes, and so forth.

Conclusion

Keep a fundamental focus on the artist of the work, not just the elements of analysis as explained in the body.

Offer a conclusion that explores the contributions of the artist in accordance with your thesis sentence.

Academic Pattern for the Analysis of History

If you are writing a history or political science paper that analyzes events and their causes and consequences, your paper should conform, in general, to the following plan. Flesh it out with the notes in your research journal to make it a working outline for drafting your paper.

Introduction

Identify the event.

Provide the background leading up to the event.

Offer quotations and paraphrases from experts.

Give the thesis sentence.

Body

Analyze the background leading up to the event.

Trace events from one historic episode to another.

Offer a chronological sequence that explains how one event relates directly to the next.

Cite authorities who have also investigated this event in history.

Conclusion

Reaffirm your thesis.

Discuss the consequences of this event.

Academic Pattern for Advancing Philosophical and Religious Ideas

If the assignment is to defend or analyze a topic from the history of ideas, use this next design, adjusting it as necessary. Make it your working outline by writing sentences and even paragraphs for each item in the model.

Introduction

Establish the idea or question.

Trace its history.

Discuss its significance.

Introduce experts who have addressed the idea.

Provide a thesis sentence that presents your approach to the issue(s)—from a fresh perspective, if at all possible.

Body

Evaluate the issues surrounding the concept.

Develop a past-to-present examination of theories.

Compare and analyze the details and minor issues.

Cite experts who have addressed this idea.

Conclusion

Advance and defend your thesis as it grows out of evidence about the idea.

Close with an effective quotation from a noted person.

Academic Pattern for the Review of a Performance

If the assignment is to review a musical, artistic, or literary performance, such as an opera, a set of paintings, a reading, a drama, or theatrical performance, adjust this next paradigm to your subject and purpose. *Note:* The review differs from the interpretation (see page 64) by its focus on evaluation rather than analysis.

Introduction

Identify the work.

Give a brief summary in one sentence.

Provide background information or history of the work.

Offer biographical facts about the artist that relate to the specific issues.

Quote and paraphrase authorities to establish the scholarly traditions that relate to this work and the performance.

Write a thesis sentence that establishes your judgment of the performance.

Body

> Offer an evaluation based on a predetermined set of criteria. Judge a drama
> by its staging and acting, music by its quality of voice and instruments,
> art by its design, literature by its themes, and so forth.

Conclusion

> Focus on the performance, the performers, and the artist.
>
> Offer a judgment based on the criteria given in the body.

Academic Pattern for Advancing Your Ideas and Theories

If you want to advance a social or legal theory in your paper, use this
design, adjusting it to eliminate unnecessary items and adding new elements as appropriate. Build this model into a working outline by assign-
ing your notes, photocopies, and downloaded files to a specific line of the
model.

Introduction

> Establish the theory, problem, or question.
>
> Discuss its significance.
>
> Provide the necessary background information.
>
> Introduce experts who have addressed the problem.
>
> Provide a thesis sentence that relates the problem to a fresh perspective.

Body

> Evaluate the issues involved in the problem.
>
> Develop a chronological examination.
>
> Compare and analyze the details and minor issues.
>
> Cite experts who have addressed the same problem.

Conclusion

> Advance and defend your theory.
>
> Discuss the implications of your findings.
>
> Offer directives or a plan of action.
>
> Suggest additional research that might be appropriate.

Academic Pattern for Argument and Persuasion Papers

If you write persuasively or argue from a set position, your paper should conform, in general, to this next paradigm. Select the elements that fit your design, begin to elaborate on them, and gradually build a frame for your paper.

Introduction

Establish clearly the problem or controversy that your paper will examine.

Summarize the issues.

Define key terminology.

Make concessions on some points of the argument.

Use quotations and paraphrases to explore the controversy.

Provide background information.

Write a thesis to establish your position.

Body

Develop arguments to defend one side of the subject.

Analyze the issues, both pro and con.

Give evidence from the sources, including quotations from the scholarship as appropriate.

Conclusion

Expand your thesis into a conclusion to demonstrate that your position has been formulated logically through careful analysis and discussion of the issues.

Academic Model for a Comparative Study

A comparative study requires that you examine two schools of thought, two issues, two works, or the positions taken by two persons. It explores similarities and differences, generally using one of three arrangements for the body of the paper. As you embellish the model you will gradually build your working outline.

Introduction

Establish A.
Establish B.

Briefly compare the two.

Introduce the central issues.

Cite source materials on the subjects.

Present your thesis.

Body (choose one)

Examine A.	Compare A and B.	Issue 1: Discuss A and B.
Examine B.	Contrast A and B.	Issue 2: Discuss A and B.
Compare and contrast A and B.	Discuss the central issues.	Issue 3: Discuss A and B.

Conclusion

Discuss the significant issues.

Rank one of the subjects over the other, or rate the respective genius of each side.

Academic Pattern for a Laboratory Investigation or Field Report

This model has little flexibility. Instructors will expect your report to remain tightly focused on each of these items.

Introduction

Provide the title, the experiment number, and the date.

Describe the experiment.

List any literature consulted.

Objectively describe what it is that you hope to accomplish.

Method

Explain the procedures used to reproduce the experiment.

Explain the design of the test.

Identify any tools or apparatus used.

Identify any variables that affected your research (weather conditions, temperatures, and so on).

Results

Give your findings, including statistical data.

Discussion

Provide your interpretation of the data.

Discuss implications to be drawn from the research.

Comment on what you learned by the experiment (optional).

Academic Pattern for Scientific Analysis

In this situation, you are working with the literature on a scientific issue, so you have more flexibility than with a report on a lab experiment.

Introduction

Identify the scientific issue or problem and state your hypothesis.

Explore the history of the topic.

Cite the literature that pertains to the topic.

Explain the purpose of the examination and its possible implications.

Body

Classify the issues.

Analyze, define, and compare each aspect of the topic.

Offer cause-effect explanations.

Make a detailed inquiry into all relevant issues.

Conclusion

Explain the current findings of scientific studies related to your topic.

Advance your reasons for continued research.

Suggest possible findings.

Discuss the implications of your analysis.

Academic Pattern for a Report of Empirical Research

This pattern is similar to the one for a laboratory investigation, so follow it closely to fill all the required items.

Introduction

Present the point of your study.

State the hypothesis and how it relates to the problem.

Provide the theoretical implications.

Explain the manner in which your study relates to previously published work.

Method

Describe the subject (what was tested, who participated—whether human or animal—and where the field work was accomplished).

Describe the apparatus to explain your equipment and how you used it.

Summarize the procedure and the execution of each stage of your work.

Results

Summarize the data you collected.

Provide statistical treatment of your findings with tables, graphs, and charts.

Include findings that conflict with your hypothesis.

Discussion

Discuss the implications of your work.

Evaluate the data and its relevance to the hypothesis.

Interpret the findings as necessary.

Discuss the implications of the findings.

Qualify the results and limit them to your specific study.

Make inferences from the results.

Suggest areas worthy of additional research.

5b Using Your Thesis to Control the Outline

After you have selected an academic pattern appropriate to your assignment, you should use your thesis sentence (or hypothesis) to set the tone and direction of your paper. Notice below how variations in the thesis can affect the arrangement of the paper.

Argument

THESIS: Misunderstandings about organ donation distort reality and set serious limits on the availability of organs to persons who need an eye, a liver, or a healthy heart.

```
Argument 1.   Many myths mislead people into
              believing that donation is
              unethical.
Argument 2.   Some fear that as a patient they
              might be put down early.
Argument 3.   Religious views sometimes get in the
              way of donation.
```

This preliminary outline gives this writer three categories for an analysis of the issues.

Cause and Effect

THESIS: Television can have positive effects on a child's language development.

```
Consequence 1. Television introduces new words.
Consequence 2. Television reinforces word usage
               and proper syntax.
Consequence 3. Literary classics come alive on
               television.
Consequence 4. Television exposes children to the
               subtle rhythms and musical effects
               of accomplished speakers.
```

Notice that the thesis on television's educational values points the way to four issues worthy of investigation.

Evaluation

THESIS: The architectural drawing for the university's new student center is not friendly to the handicapped.

```
Evaluation 1.   The common areas seem cramped and
                narrow, with few open areas in
                which students can cluster.
Evaluation 2.   Steps and stairs seem all too
                common in the design.
Evaluation 3.   Only one elevator appears in the
                plans when three would be fair and
                equitable.
```

Evaluation 4. Only the first-floor rest rooms
offer universal access.

Evaluation 5. The parking spaces designated for
people with physical handicaps are
located at an entrance with steps,
not a ramp.

This outline evolves from a thesis sentence that invites evaluation
of an architectural plan.

Comparison

THESIS: Discipline often involves punishment, but
child abuse adds another element: the
gratification of the adult.

Comparison 1. A spanking has the interest of the
child at heart, but a beating or a
caning has no redeeming value.

Comparison 2. Time-outs remind the child that
relationships are important and to
be cherished, but lockouts in a
closet only promote hysteria and
fear.

Comparison 3. The parent's ego and selfish
interests often take precedence
over the welfare of the child or
children.

This thesis sentence motivates a pattern of comparison by which to
judge the relative differences between punishment of a child and child
abuse.

5c Writing an Outline

Not all papers require a complete, formal outline, nor do all researchers
need one. A short research paper can be created from keywords, a list
of issues, a rough outline, and a first draft. However, an outline sometimes is important, for it fleshes out the academic pattern you have
selected (see section 5a) by classifying the issues of your study into clear,

logical categories with main headings and one or more levels of sub-headings.

A formal outline is not rigid and inflexible; you may, and should, modify it while writing and revising. In every case, treat an outline or organizational chart as a tool. Like an architect's blueprint, it should contribute to, not inhibit, the construction of a finished product. You may wish to experiment with the Outline feature of your software, which allows you to view the paper at various levels of detail and to highlight and drop the essay into a different organization.

Topic Outline

Build a topic outline of balanced phrases. You can use noun phrases ("the rods of the retina"), gerund phrases ("sensing dim light with retina rods"), or infinitive phrases ("to sense dim light with retina rods"). No matter which grammatical format you choose, follow it consistently throughout the outline. One student used noun phrases to outline her scientific analysis:

```
 I.Diabetes defined
    A.A disease without control
       1.A disorder of the metabolism
       2.The search for a cure
    B.Types of diabetes
       1.Type 1, juvenile diabetes
       2.Type 2, adult onset diabetes
 II. Health complications
    A.The problem of hyperglycemia
       1.Signs and symptoms of the problem
       2.Lack of insulin
    B.The conflict of the kidneys and the liver
       1.Effects of ketoacidosis
       2.Effects of arteriosclerosis
III.   Proper care and control
    A.Blood sugar monitoring
       1.Daily monitoring at home
       2.Hemoglobin test at a laboratory
    B.Medication for diabetes
```

            1. Insulin injections
            2. Hypoglycemia agents
        C. Exercise programs
            1. Walking
            2. Swimming
            3. Aerobic workouts
        D. Diet and meal planning
            1. Exchange plan
            2. Carbohydrate counting
    IV. Conclusion: Balance of all the factors

Sentence Outline

Instead of an outline with phrases, you may use full sentences for each heading and subheading. Using sentences has two advantages over the topic outline: (1) Many entries in a sentence outline can serve as topic sentences for paragraphs, thereby accelerating the writing process, and (2) The subject-verb pattern establishes the logical direction of your thinking (for example, the phrase *Vocabulary development* becomes *Television viewing can improve a child's vocabulary*). Note below a brief portion of one student's sentence outline.

    I. Organ and tissue donation is the gift of life.
        A. Organs that can be successfully transplanted
            include the heart, lungs, liver, kidneys, and
            pancreas.
        B. Tissues that can be transplanted successfully
            include bone, corneas, skin, heart valves, veins,
            cartilage, and other connective tissues.
        C. The process of becoming a donor is easy.
        D. Many people receive organ and tissue transplants
            each year, but still many people die because they
            did not receive the needed transplant.

Your Research Project

1. Scratch out an outline for your project. List your general thesis and below that establish several divisions that will require careful and full

development. Test more than one plan. Do you need several criteria of judgment? causal issues? arguments? evidence from field research? Which seems to work best for you?

2. Select one of the paradigms, as found on pages 63–71, and develop academic model fully with the information from your rough outline (see #1 above).

CHAPTER SIX

FINDING AND READING THE BEST SOURCES

Finding sources worthy of citation in your paper can be a challenge. This chapter cuts to the heart of the matter: How do you find the best, most appropriate sources? Should you read all or just part of a source? How do you respond to it? Also, in this age of electronic publications, you must constantly review and verify to your own satisfaction the words of your sources. It is wise to consider every article on the Internet as suspect unless you access it through your library's databases. See pages 50–51 for guidelines on judging the value of Internet articles.

6a   Understanding the Assignment

A general search for sources on the Internet may serve your needs for writing a short paper, but the research paper requires you to compose from books, scholarly journals, and academic articles. Also, a specific academic discipline usually controls your research. For example, an assignment to examine the recreational programs at selected day care centers requires research in the literature of the social sciences found at your library's electronic catalogs rather than the Internet.

Primary and Secondary Sources

In addition, you need a mix of primary and secondary sources. *Primary sources* include novels, speeches, eyewitness accounts, interviews, letters, autobiographies, observation during field research, or the written results of empirical research. You should feel free to quote often from a primary source that has direct relevance to your discussion. For example, if you present a poem by Dylan Thomas, you should quote the poem. *Secondary sources* are writings about the primary sources, about an author, or about somebody's accomplishments. Secondary sources include a report on a presidential speech, a review of new scientific findings, analysis of a poem, or a biography of a notable person. These evaluations, analyses, and interpretations provide ways of looking at original, primary sources. Here's a guide to sources for the major disciplines.

Guide to Academic Sources

Humanities *Primary sources* in literature and the fine arts are novels, poems, and plays as well as films, paintings, music, and sculpture. Your task is to examine, interpret, and evaluate these original works. Researchers in history must look at speeches, documents written by historic figures, and some government documents.

Secondary sources in the humanities are evaluations in journal articles and books, critical reviews, biographies, and history books.

Field research in the humanities will require interviews with an artist or government official, letters, e-mail surveys, online discussion groups, and the archival study of manuscripts.

Social Sciences *Primary sources* in education, political science, psychology, and other fields include speeches, writings by presidents and others, documents recorded in the *Congressional Record*, reports and statistics of government agencies and departments, and papers at your state's archival library.

Field research is most important in the social sciences and consists of case studies, findings from surveys and questionnaires, tests and test data, interviews, and observation. In business reports, field research consists of market testing, drawings and designs, industrial research, letters, and interviews.

Secondary sources include books and articles on social, political, and psychological issues, analyses and evaluations in journal articles, discussions of the business world in newspapers, magazines, and journals, and—in general—anything written about key personalities, events, products, and primary documents.

Sciences *Primary sources* in the sciences consist of the words and theories of scientists discussing natural phenomena or offering their views on scientific issues, such as the words of Charles Darwin or Stephen Hawking. At the same time, journal articles that report on empirical research are considered primary material because they are original in their testing of a hypothesis.

Secondary sources in the sciences are not abundant. They appear generally as review articles that discuss testing and experiments by several scientists—for example, the review of four or five articles on gene mutation.

Field research and laboratory testing are crucial to the sciences and provide the results of experiments, discoveries, tests, and observations.

6b Identifying the Best Source Materials

Let's look at an inverted pyramid that shows you a progression from excellent sources to less reliable ones. The chart does not ask you to ignore or dismiss items at the bottom, such as magazines and e-mail discussion groups, but it lets you know when to feel confident and when to be on guard about the validity of the source.

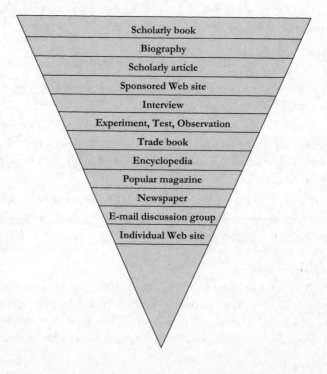

Scholarly book
Biography
Scholarly article
Sponsored Web site
Interview
Experiment, Test, Observation
Trade book
Encyclopedia
Popular magazine
Newspaper
E-mail discussion group
Individual Web site

Scholarly Book

Scholarly books, including textbooks, treat academic topics with in-depth discussions and careful documentation of the evidence. A college library is a repository for scholarly books—technical and scientific works, doctoral dissertations, publications of the university presses, and many textbooks. Scholarly books are subjected to careful review before publication, and they are published because they give the very best treatment of a subject. However, in the sciences, books grow out of date quickly, so depend on monthly journals to keep your research current.

Biography

The library's electronic catalog can help you find an appropriate biography from among the thousands available; representative databases include *Contemporary Authors* and *Dictionary of American Negro Biography*. You can also learn about a notable person on the Internet by searching for the name of the person and carefully scanning the sites that are returned. Notable persons are likely to have a Web site devoted to them. A *critical biography* is a book devoted not only to the life of the subject but also to his or her life's work; an excellent example is Richard Ellmann's *Oscar Wilde*, a critical study of Wilde's writings as well as his life.

You may need a biography for several reasons:

- To verify the standing and reputation of somebody you want to paraphrase or quote in your paper.

- To provide biographical details in your introduction. For example, the primary topic may be Carl Jung's psychological theories of the unconscious, but information about Jung's career might also be appropriate in the paper.

- To discuss a creative writer's life in relation to his or her work—that is, details of Joyce Carol Oates's personal life may illuminate your reading of her stories and novels.

Scholarly Article

Scholarly articles are best found through one of the library's databases (see pages 19–25). The academic database takes you to journal articles or articles at academically sponsored Web sites. You can feel confident about the authenticity of journal articles because the authors write for academic honor, document all sources, and publish through university presses and academic organizations. Thus, a journal article about child abuse found in *Journal of Marriage and the Family* or found through the PsychINFO database may be considered reliable. Nevertheless, some popular magazines are noted for their quality, such as *Atlantic Monthly, Scientific Review,* and *Discover.* The major newspapers—*New York Times, Atlanta Journal-Constitution,* and *Wall Street Journal*—often hire the best writers and columnists, so valuable articles can be found in both printed and online newspapers.

Sponsored Web Site

The Internet supplies both excellent and dubious information. You must be careful when evaluating Web materials. Chapter 3 explores research on the Web. In addition to the checklist on pages 50–51, "Evaluating Internet Sources," you should also ask yourself a few questions about any Web site information:

- Is it appropriate to my work?
- Does it reveal a serious and scholarly emphasis?
- Is it sponsored by a professional institution or organization?

Interview

Interviews with knowledgeable people provide excellent information for a research paper. Whether conducted in person, by telephone, or by e-mail, the interview brings a personal, expert perspective to your work. The key element, of course, is the experience of the person. For full details about conducting an interview, see pages 55–56.

Experiment, Test, or Observation

Gathering your own data for research is a staple in many fields, especially the sciences. An experiment will bring primary evidence into your paper as you explain your hypothesis, give the test results, and discuss the implications of your findings. For details on the format for a scientific investigation see pages 60–62.

Trade Book

How to Launch a Small Business and *Landscaping with Rocks* are typical titles of nonfiction trade books found in bookstores rather than college libraries (although public libraries often have trade book holdings). Designed for commercial consumption, trade books seldom treat a scholarly subject in depth. Unlike scholarly books and textbooks, manuscripts for trade books do not go through the rigors of peer review. For example, if your topic is dieting, with a focus on fad diets, you will find plenty of diet books at the local bookstore and numerous articles on commercial Web sites. However, serious discussions backed by careful research are found in the journals or at sponsored Web sites.

Encyclopedia

An encyclopedia, by design, contains brief surveys of every well-known person, event, place, and accomplishment. It will serve your preliminary investigation for a topic, but most instructors prefer that you go beyond encyclopedias to cite from scholarly books and journal articles. However, specialized encyclopedias (see pages 25–28) often have in-depth articles by noted scholars.

Popular Magazine

Like a trade book, a magazine article seldom offers in-depth information and does not face the critical review of a panel of experts. Thus, you must exercise caution when using it as a source. In general, college libraries house the better magazines—those that have merit in the quality of writing—so depend on the library's list of academic databases. For example, if your paper concerns sports medicine, citing an article from the *Atlantic Monthly* or *Scientific Review* will gain you far higher marks than one from *Sports Illustrated*, *Sport*, or *NBA Basketball*.

Newspaper

Newspaper reporters write under the pressure of deadlines. They do not have as much time to do careful research as do writers of journal articles. On occasion, a newspaper will assign reporters to a series of articles on a complex topic, and such in-depth analyses have merit. As noted above, the major newspapers—*New York Times, Atlanta Journal-Constitution,* and *Wall Street Journal*—often hire highly qualified writers and columnists, so valuable articles can be found in both the printed and online versions of these papers. You must remember, however, that newspaper articles, like those in magazines and on the Internet, must receive cautionary and critical evaluation.

E-mail Discussion Group

E-mail information via a forum established by the instructor for an course deserves consideration when it focuses on academic issues such as British Romantic literature or, more specifically, Shelley's poetry. In some cases, they originate for students in an online course, providing a venue for sharing ideas. However, rather than search for quotable material from e-mail forums, use them as a sounding board to generate ideas and test them with other participants.

Individual Web Site

A person's home page, with its various links to other information, provides a publication medium for anybody who may or may not possess knowledge. You cannot avoid them because they pop up on various search engines. You should approach them with caution. For example, one student, investigating the topic *fad diets* searched the Web to find mostly home pages that described personal battles with weight loss or commercial sites that were blatant in their attempts to sell something. Caution becomes vital.

Internet Chat Conversations

Real-time Internet conversations have almost no value for academic research and are not legitimate sources for your paper. Seldom do you know the participants beyond their usernames, and the conversations seldom focus on scholarly issues.

6c   Evaluating a Source

Confronted by several books and articles, many writers have trouble determining the value of material and the contribution it can make to the research paper. To save time, you must be selective in your reading. To serve your reader, you must cite carefully selected material that is pertinent to the argument. Avoid dumping huge blocks of quotation into the paper because the paper will lose your style and the personal flavor of your own voice. You must be concerned about the relevance, authority, accuracy, and currency of all sources you cite in your paper.

Relevance

To determine how well an article or book fits the demands of your research, skim it. For a periodical or Internet article, examine the title, the abstract or introduction, and both the opening and closing paragraphs.

Authority

To test the authority of a source, examine the credentials of the author (usually found in a brief biographical profile or note of professional affiliation) and the sponsoring institution—usually the publisher of a journal, such as the American Sociological Association, or the sponsor of a Web site, such as **http://www.ucla.edu**. Look at the bibliography at the end of the article, for it signals the scholarly nature of the work and also points you toward other material on this subject. Study the home page of an Internet article, if there is one. Prefer sites sponsored by universities and professional organizations. Note hypertext links to other sites whose quality may be determined by the domain tags, such as .edu, .org, and .gov. Be wary of .com sites. See pages 50–51 for guidelines on judging the value of Internet articles.

Note: The *definitive edition* of a work is the most reliable version of a play, novel, or collection of poems; it is definitive because it is the one the author supervised through the press. The way an author wanted the work presented can be found only in a definitive edition. Thus, electronic versions usually do not display the original author's page and type design, unless they are photocopies of the original, as at the JSTOR site (see page 23).

Accuracy

In the sciences, scholars talk about the verification of an article, which means they can, if necessary, replicate the research and the findings. A scientific report must carefully detail the design of the work, the methods, subjects, and procedures. A lab experiment, for example, should repeat previous findings to demonstrate accuracy. The writer should reveal the details of a control group, an experimental group, and the testing procedures. Any scientific report that does not establish research methods should not be cited.

Currency

Use recent sources for research in the sciences and social sciences. A psychology book may look valuable, but if its copyright date is 1955 the content has probably been replaced by recent research and current developments. When reading a source, be certain at least one date is listed. Electronic publications sometimes show the site has been updated or refreshed, but the article itself may carry an older date. On the Internet, check the date of print publication; it may be different than that of the Web publication. As a general rule, use the most recent date for an article on the Internet, which means you could list as many as three dates—the year of the print publication, the most recent year of the Internet publication, and the date you accessed the material.

Your Research Project

1. Examine your sources to test the validity of the list against the inverted pyramid on page 79. Do you have enough sources from the upper tier of scholarly works? If not, go in search of journal articles and scholarly books to beef up the list. Do not depend entirely upon Internet articles, even if each appears on sponsored Web site.

2. Examine your sources to establish a balance of primary and secondary sources. Look for your discipline—literature, government, history—and then determine if you are using a mix of primary and secondary sources

3. Respond to one of your sources by writing two items: (1) a rough outline of the contents of the source and (2) a brief summary of the source.

CHAPTER SEVEN

WRITING
EFFECTIVE NOTES

Notetaking is the heart of research. If you write notes of high quality, they may need only minor editing to fit the appropriate places in your first draft. Prepare yourself to write different types of notes—quotations for well-phrased passages by authorities but also paraphrased or summarized notes to maintain your voice. This chapter explains the following types of notes:

- *Personal notes* that express your own ideas or record field research.
- *Quotation notes* that preserve the distinguished syntax of an authority.
- *Paraphrase notes* that interpret and restate what the authority has said.
- *Summary notes* that capture in capsule form a writer's ideas.
- *Field notes* that record interviews, tabulate questionnaires, and maintain records of laboratory experiments and other types of field research.

Honoring the Conventions of Research Style

Essential to your effectiveness in notetaking is to honor the conventions of research style. Your notes will be more effective from the start if you practice MLA (Modern Language Association) style for citing a source within your text. This citation style stresses the name of the source and the page number when available.

```
Lawrence Smith states, "The suicidal teen causes
severe damage to the psychological condition of
peers" (34).
```

CHECKLIST WRITING EFFECTIVE NOTES

1. Write each note in a separate, labeled file within one folder, although you can keep several notes in one computer file if each is labeled clearly. Remember, downloaded files from Internet databases must also be labeled clearly.

2. Accompany each file with the name, year, and page of the source to prepare for in-text citations.

3. Label each file (for example, *objectivity on television*).

4. Write a full note in well-developed sentences to speed the writing of your first draft.

5. Keep everything (photocopy, scribbled note) in order to authenticate dates, page numbers, and full names.

6. Label your personal notes with *my idea* or *personal note* to distinguish them from the sources.

7a Writing Personal Notes

The content of a research paper is an expression of your own ideas as supported by the scholarly evidence. It is not a collection of ideas transmitted by experts in books and articles. Readers are primarily interested in *your* thesis sentence, *your* topic sentences, and *your* personal view of the issues. Therefore, during your research, record your thoughts on the issues by writing plenty of personal notes in your research journal and computer files. Personal notes are essential because they allow you to record your discoveries, reflect on the findings, make connections, and identify the prevailing views and patterns of thought. Remember two standards: (1) The idea written into the file is yours, and (2) the file is labeled with *my idea, mine, personal thought* to distinguish it from information borrowed from a source. Here's an example:

```
Personal thought
    For me, organ donation might be a gift of life, so
I have signed my donor card. At least a part of me
will continue to live if an accident claims my life.
My boyfriend says I'm gruesome, but I consider it
```

```
practical. Besides, he might be the one who benefits,
and then what will he say?
```

7b Writing Direct Quotation Notes

Quotation notes are essential because they allow you to capture the authoritative voices of the experts on the topic, feature well-phrased statements, offer conflicting points of view, and share the literature on the topic with your readers. Follow these basic conventions.

1. Select material that is important and well-phrased, not something trivial or something that is common knowledge. Not "John F. Kennedy was a Democrat from Massachusetts" (Rupert 233) but this:

   ```
   "John F. Kennedy's Peace Corps left a legacy of
   lasting compassion for the downtrodden"(Rupert 233).
   ```

2. Use quotation marks around the quoted material in your notes, working draft, and final manuscript. Do not copy or download the words of a source into your paper in such a way that readers will think you wrote the material.

3. Use the exact words of the source.

4. Provide an appropriate in-text citation, as in this note:

   ```
   Griffiths, Kilman, and Frost suggest that the
   killing of architect Stanford White in 1904 was
   "the beginning of the most bitterly savage century
   known to mankind" (113). Murder, wars, and human
   atrocities were the "sad vestiges" of an era that
   had great promise.
   ```

5. The parenthetical citation goes *outside* the final quotation mark but *inside* the period for quotations within your sentence. Block quotations require a different setup (see page 91).

6. Quote key sentences and short passages, not entire paragraphs. Find the essential statement and feature it; do not force your reader to read a long quoted passage that has only one statement relevant to your point. Make the essential idea a part of your sentence, as shown here:

```
Many Americans, trying to mend their past eating
habits, adopt functional foods as an essential step
toward a more health-conscious future. Balthrop
says this group of believers spends "an estimated
$29 billion a year" on functional foods (6).
```

7. Quote from both primary sources (the original words of a writer or speaker) and secondary sources (comments after the fact about original works). The two types are discussed immediately below.

Quoting the Primary Sources

Quote from primary sources for four reasons:

- To draw on the wisdom of the original author
- To let readers hear the precise words of the author
- To copy exact lines of poetry and drama
- To reproduce graphs, charts, and statistical data

Cite poetry, fiction, drama, letters, and interviews. In other cases, you may want to quote liberally from a presidential speech, cite the words of a business executive, or reproduce original data.

Quoting the Secondary Sources

Quote from secondary sources for three reasons:

- To display excellence in ideas and expression by experts on the topic
- To explain complex material
- To set up a statement of your own, especially if it spins off, adds to, or takes exception to the source as quoted

The overuse of direct quotation from secondary sources indicates either (1) that you did not have a clear focus and copied verbatim just about everything related to the subject, or (2) that you had inadequate evidence and used numerous quotations as padding. Therefore, limit quotations from secondary sources by using only a phrase or a sentence:

```
Reginald Herman says the geographical changes in
Russia require "intensive political analysis" (15).
```

If you quote an entire sentence, make the quotation a direct object that tells *what* the authority says.

```
In response to the changes in Russia, one critic
notes, "The American government must exercise
caution and conduct intensive political analysis"
(15).
```

7c Writing Paraphrased Notes

A paraphrase requires you to restate in your own words the thought, meaning, and attitude of someone else. Your interpretation acts as a bridge between the source and the reader as you capture the wisdom of the source in approximately the same number of words. Use paraphrase to maintain your voice or style in the paper, to avoid an endless string of direct quotations, and to interpret the source as you rewrite it. Keep in mind these five rules for paraphrasing a source:

1. Rewrite the original in about the same number of words.
2. Provide an in-text citation to the source (in MLA style, the author and page number).
3. Retain exceptional words and phrases from the original by enclosing them in quotation marks.
4. Preserve the tone of the original by suggesting moods of satire, anger, humor, doubt, and so on. Show the author's attitude with appropriate verbs: "Omar Tavares condemns . . . defends . . . argues . . . explains . . . observes . . . defines."
5. Put the original aside while paraphrasing to avoid copying word for word. Compare the finished paraphrase with the original source to be certain that the paraphrase truly rewrites the original and that it uses quotation marks with any phrasing or key words retained from the original.

HINT: When instructors see an in-text citation but no quotation marks, they will assume that you are paraphrasing, not quoting. Be sure their assumption is correct.

Here are examples that show the differences between a quotation note and a paraphrased one:

Quotation:

Hein explains heredity in this way: "Except for
identical twins, each person's heredity is unique"
(294).

Paraphrase:

One source explains that heredity is special and
distinct for each of us, unless a person is one of
identical twins (Hein 294).

Quotation (block indent of four lines or more):

Hein explains the phenomenon in this way:
        Since only half of each parent's chromosomes
    are transmitted to a child and since this
    half represents a chance selection of those
    the child could inherit, only twins that
    develop from a single fertilized egg that
    splits in two have identical chromosomes.
    (294)

Paraphrase:

Hein specifies that twins have identical
chromosomes because they grow from one egg that
divides after it has been fertilized. He affirms
that most brothers and sisters differ because of
the "chance selection" of chromosomes transmitted
by each parent (294).

As shown in the example immediately above, place any key wording of the source within quotation marks.

7d Writing Summary Notes

A summary of a source serves a specific purpose, so it deserves a polished style for transfer into the paper. It requires you to capture in just a few words the ideas of an entire paragraph, section, or chapter. Store it in your folder with its own file name. It may be a rough sketch of the source or a polished note. Use it for these reasons:

- To review an article or book
- To annotate a bibliography entry
- To provide a plot summary
- To create an abstract

Success with the summary requires the following:

1. Condense the original content with precision and directness. Reduce a long paragraph to a sentence, tighten an article into a brief paragraph, and summarize a book in a page.

2. Preserve the tone of the original. If the original is serious, suggest that tone in the summary. In the same way, retain moods of doubt, skepticism, optimism, and so forth.

3. Write the summary in your own language; however, retain exceptional phrases from the original, enclosing them in quotation marks.

4. Provide documentation.

Use the Summary to Review Briefly an Article or Book

Note this example, which reviews two entire articles:

> Alec Twobears has two closely related articles on
> this subject, and both, one in 2001 and another in
> 2002, are about the failure of the United States to
> follow through with the treaties it signed with the
> Indian nations of North America. He opens both with
> "No treaty is a good treaty!" He signals clearly
> the absence of trust by native Americans toward the
> government in Washington, DC.

To see more summaries of this type, presented in a review of the literature, see pages 98–109.

Use the Summary to Write an Annotated Bibliography

An annotation offers a brief explanation or critical commentary on an article or book. Thus, an annotated bibliography is one in which each source is followed immediately by the annotation, as shown here in MLA style.

"Top Ten Myths about Donation and Transplantation."
TransWeb Webcast, 2002. 10 Oct. 2003 <http://www.
transweb.org/news/htm>. This site dispels the many
myths surrounding organ donation, showing that selling organs is illegal, that matching donor and
recipient is highly complicated, and secret back room
operations are almost impossible.

See pages 95–98 to view more annotated bibliography entries.

Use the Summary in a Plot Summary Note

In just a few sentences, a summary can describe a novel, short story, drama, or similar literary work, as shown by this next note:

Great Expectations by Dickens describes young Pip,
who inherits money and can live the life of a
gentleman. But he discovers that his "great
expectations" have come from a criminal. With that
knowledge his attitude changes from one of vanity
to one of compassion.

Use the Summary to Create an Abstract

An abstract is a brief description that appears at the beginning of an article to summarize the contents. Usually, it is written by the article's author,
and it helps readers make decisions about reading the entire article. You
can find entire volumes devoted to abstracts, such as *Psychological
Abstracts* and *Abstracts of English Studies*. An abstract is required for
most papers in the social and natural sciences. Here's a sample from
one student's paper:

                    Abstract
Functional foods, products that provide benefits
beyond basic nutrition, are adding billions to the
nation's economy each year. Functional foods are
suspected to be a form of preventive medicine.
Consumers hope that functional foods can calm some
.of their medical anxieties, while researchers
believe that functional foods may lower health care

costs. The paper identifies several functional
foods, locates the components that make them work,
and explains the role that each plays on the body.

7e   Writing Notes from Field Research

For some research projects, you will be expected to conduct field research.
This work may require different kinds of notes kept on charts, cards,
notepads, laboratory notebooks, a research journal, or the computer.
Interviews require careful notetaking during the session and dutiful tran-
scription of those notes to your draft. A tape recorder can serve as a
backup to your notetaking. A questionnaire produces valuable data for
developing notes and graphs and charts for your research paper.

The procedures and findings of experiments, tests, and
measurements serve as your notes for the Method and Results
sections of the report. Here is an example of one student's laboratory
notebook—a passage he might transfer to the Procedures section of his
paper:

First, 25.0 ml of a vinegar sample was delivered to
a 50-ml volumetric flask, with a 25-ml pipet, and
diluted to the mark with distilled water. It was
mixed thoroughly and 50.00-ml aliquot were emptied
into three 250-ml conical flasks, with a 25-ml
pipet, 50 ml of distilled water, and two drops of
phenolphthalein were added to each of the flasks.
The samples were then titrated with a .345 M NaOH
solution until the first permanent pink color.

7f   Using Your Notes to Write
an Annotated Bibliography

Writing an annotated bibliography may look like busywork, but it helps you
evaluate the strength and nature of your sources. The annotated bibliography that follows is written in MLA style. An *annotation* is a summary
of the contents of a book or article. A *bibliography* is a list of sources
on a selected topic. Thus, an annotated bibliography does two important things: (1) it lists bibliographic data for a selection of sources, and
(2) it summarizes the contents of each book or article.

The annotated bibliography that follows summarizes a few sources on the issue of tanning, tanning beds, lotions, and the dangers of skin cancer.

Levenson 1

Norman Levenson
Professor Davidson
English 1020
24 October 2005

Annotated Bibliography

Brown, Edwin W. "Tanning Beds and the 'Safe Tan' Myth." <u>Medical Update</u> 21 (1998): 6. Brown makes the point that there is "no such thing as a 'safe' or 'healthy' tan. " He explains that tanning is the skin's reaction to radiation damage, and "tanned skin is damaged skin." He cautions that tans from tanning beds are no different than those produced by the sun. Like others, he encourages the use of SPF 15 or higher.

Cohen, Russell. "Tanning Trouble: Teens Are Using Tanning Beds in Record Numbers." <u>Scholastic Choices</u> 18 (2003): 23-28. Cohen warns that tanning beds "can be just as dangerous as the sun's rays" (23). The writer explains that tanning salons are not well regulated, so the amount of exposure can be really dangerous. The

Each entry gives full bibliographic information on the source— author, title, and publication data—as well as a brief description of the article or book.

Levenson 2

writer also explains how skin type
affects tanning and the dangers of
cancer.

Geller, Alan C., et al. "Use of Sunscreen,
    Sunburning Rates, and Tanning Bed Use
    among More Than 10,000 U.S. Children
    and Adolescents." Pediatrics 109
    (2002): 1009-15. The objective of this
    study was to examine the psychosocial
    variables associated with teens
    seeking suntans. It collected data
    from questionnaires submitted by
    10,079 boys and girls 12 to 18 years
    old. It concluded that many children
    are at risk for skin cancer because of
    failure to use sunscreen.

Segilia, Amanda. "Sunscreens, Suntans, and
    Sun Health." American Cancer Society.
    Interview. 13 June 2000. 4 June 2003
    <http://www.intelihealth.com/search>.
    This site features Harvard Medical
    School's Consumer Health Information. In
    this article, Amanda Segilia, a
    coordinator of Cancer Control Programs
    for the American Cancer Society, answers
    questions about tanning, including the
    use of sunscreen of SPF 15 or higher,
    use of suntan lotions, the effects of
    the sun, and the dangers of skin
    cancer.

"Skin Protection—My Teen Likes to Tan." St.
    Louis Children's Hospital. 2003. 22

Levenson 3

Oct. 2005 <http://www.stlouischildrens.
org/articles/article_print.
asp?ID=2670>. This site quotes Susan
Mallory, the director of dermatology at
St. Louis Children's Hospital, and
registered nurse Ann Leonard, who both
offer warnings against the use of
tanning beds. Rather than damaging the
skin with sun or tanning beds, the two
experts suggest the use of tanning
sprays or lotions.
"Teens and the Sun." Health Watch. The U
of Texas Southwestern Medical Center at
Dallas. 29 July 2002. 21 Oct. 2005
<http://www3.utsouthwestern.edu/
library/consumer/teen&sun02.htm>. This
article warns teenagers against sun
worship and skipping sunscreen. The
experts suggest more public education
and warnings. For example, teens should
know that tanning damages the structure
of the skin and promotes sagging skin
and wrinkles in later life.
Zazinski, Janice. "A Legion of Ladies'
Lesions." Research Briefs. Boston U.
11 Aug. 2000. 21 Oct. 2005 <www.bu.
edu/news/research/2000/8-11-suntans-
chf.htm>. This article cites Dr.
Marie-France Demierre, a professor of
dermatology, who laments the use of
tanning beds by young women. In truth,
women are joining men in contracting

Levenson 4

and dying of melanoma, in great part
because of tanning beds. Demierre and
Zazinski warn youngsters against
addiction to tanning beds and sun
worship.

7g Using Your Notes to Write a Review of the Literature

The review of literature presents a set of summaries in essay form for two purposes.

1. It helps you investigate the topic because it forces you to examine and then to record how each source addresses the problem.

2. It organizes and classifies the sources in some reasonable manner for the benefit of the reader.

Thus, you should relate each source to your central subject, and you should group the sources according to their support of your thesis. For example, the brief review that follows explores the literature on the subject of gender communication. It classifies the sources under a progression of headings: the issues, the causes (both environmental and biological), the consequences for both men and women, and possible solutions.

You must also arrange the sources according to your selected categories or to fit your preliminary outline. Sometimes this task might be as simple as grouping those sources that favor a course or action and those that oppose it. In other cases—let's say it's a paper on Fitzgerald's *The Great Gatsby*—you may need to summarize sources by critics who examine Gatsby's character, others who study Daisy, and still others who write about Nick Carraway.

Like Kaci Holz, who wrote the paper below, you may wish to use side heads to identify your sections.

Holz 1

Kaci Holz
Dr. Bekus
April 23, 2005
English 1010

Gender Communication:
A Review of the Literature

Several theories exist about different male and female communication styles. These ideas have been categorized below to establish the issues, shows causes for communication failures, the consequences for both men and women, and suggestions for possible solutions.

The review of literature is an essay on the articles and books that address the writer's topic.

The Issues

Deborah Tannen, Ph.D., is a professor of sociolinguistics at Georgetown University. In her book <u>You Just Don't Understand: Men and Women in Conversation</u>, 1990, she claims there are basic gender patterns or stereotypes that can be found. Tannen says that men participate in conversations to establish "a hierarchical social order," while women most often participate in conversations to establish "a network of connections" (Tannen, <u>Don't Understand</u> 24–25). She distinguishes between the way

The writer uses the sources to establish the issues.

women use "rapport-talk" and the way men use "report-talk" (74).

In similar fashion, Susan Basow and Kimberly Rubenfeld, in "'Troubles Talk': Effects of Gender and Gender Typing," explore in detail the sex roles and how they determine and often control the speech of each gender. They notice that "women may engage in 'troubles talk' to enhance communication; men may avoid such talk to enhance autonomy and dominance" (186).

In addition, Phillip Yancey asserts that men and women "use conversation for quite different purposes" (71). He provides a 'no' answer to the question in his title, "Do Men and Women Speak the Same Language?" He claims that women converse to develop and maintain connections, while men converse to claim their position in the hierarchy they see around them. Yancey asserts that women are less likely to speak publicly than are men because women often perceive such speaking as putting oneself on display. A man, on the other hand, is usually comfortable with speaking publicly because that is how he establishes his status among others (Yancey 71).

Similarly, masculine people are "less likely than androgynous individuals to feel grateful for advice" (Basow and Rubenfeld 186). Julia T. Wood's book <u>Gendered Lives</u> claims that "male communication is

Holz 3

characterized by assertion, independence, competitiveness, and confidence [while] female communication is characterized by deference, inclusivity, collaboration, and cooperation" (440). This list of differences describes why men and women have such opposing communication styles.

In another book, Tannen addresses the issue that boys, or men, "are more likely to take an oppositional stance toward other people and the world" and "are more likely to find opposition entertaining—to enjoy watching a good fight, or having one" (Tannen, <u>Argument</u> 166). Girls try to avoid fights.

Causes

Two different theories suggest causes for gender differences—the environment and biology.

<u>Environmental Causes</u>. Tammy James and Bethann Cinelli in 2003 mention, "The way men and women are raised contributes to differences in conversation and communication . . . " (41). Another author, Susan Witt, in "Parental Influence on Children's Socialization to Gender Roles," discusses the various findings that support the idea that parents have a great influence on their children during the development of their self-concept. She states, "Children learn at a very early age what it means to

The writer now uses the sources to explain the causes for communication failures.

Holz 4

be a boy or a girl in our society" (253). She
says that parents "[dress] infants in gender-
specific colors, [give] gender-differentiated
toys, and [expect] different behavior from
boys and girls" (Witt 254).

Yancey notices a cultural gap, defining
culture as "shared meaning" (68). He says,
"Some problems come about because one spouse
enters marriage with a different set of
'shared meanings' than the other" (69). The
cultural gap affects the children. Yancey
also talks about the "Battle of the Sexes" as
seen in conflict between men and women.
Reverting back to his 'childhood gender
pattern' theory, Yancey claims, "Men, who
grew up in a hierarchical environment, are
accustomed to conflict. Women, concerned more
with relationship and connection, prefer the
role of peacemaker" (71).

Like Yancey, Deborah Tannen also
addresses the fact that men and women often
come from different worlds and different
influences. She says, "Even if they grow up
in the same neighborhood, on the same block,
or in the same house, girls and boys grow up
in different worlds of words" (Tannen, Don't
Understand 43).

Biological Causes. Though Tannen often
addresses the environmental issue in much of
her research, she also looks at the
biological issue in her book The Argument
Culture. Tannen states, "Surely a biological

Holz 5

component plays a part in the greater use of
antagonism among men, but cultural influence
can override biological inheritance"
(Tannen, <u>Argument</u> 205). She sums up the
nature versus nurture issue by saying, "The
patterns that typify women's and men's
styles of opposition and conflict are the
result of both biology and culture" (207).

Lillian Glass, another linguistics
researcher, has a 1992 book called <u>He Says,</u>
<u>She Says: Closing the Communication Gap</u>
<u>between the Sexes</u>. Glass addresses the issue
that different hormones found in men and
women's bodies make them act differently and
therefore communicate differently. She also
discusses how brain development has been
found to relate to sex differences.

Judy Mann says, "Most experts now
believe that what happens to boys and girls
is a complex interaction between slight
biological differences and tremendously
powerful social forces that begin to
manifest themselves the minute the parents
find out whether they are going to have a
boy or a girl" (qtd. in McCluskey 6).

Consequences of Gender Differences

Now that we have looked at different
styles of gender communication and possible
causes of gender communication, let us look
at the possible results. Michelle Weiner-
Davis is a marriage and family therapist who

*The writer now
uses the
sources to
explain the
consequence of
communication
failures on
both men and
women.*

Holz 6

wrote the best seller <u>Divorce Busting</u>. She
says to the point, "Ignorance about the
differences in gender communication has been
a major contributor to divorce" (qtd. in
Warren 106).

Through various studies, Tannen has
concluded that men and women have different
purposes for engaging in communication. In
the open forum that Deborah Tannen and
Robert Bly gave in New York in 1993, Tannen
(on videotape) explains the different ways
men and women handle communication
throughout the day. She explains
that a man constantly talks during his
workday in order to impress those around him
and to establish his status in the office.
At home he wants peace and quiet. On the
other hand, a woman is constantly cautious
and guarded about what she says during her
workday. Women try hard to avoid
confrontation and avoid offending anyone
with their language. So when a woman comes
home from work she expects to be able to
talk freely without having to guard her
words. The consequence? The woman expects
conversation, but the man is tired of
talking.

The writer now depends on the sources to provide possible solutions.

Solutions

Answers for better gender communication
seem elusive. What can be done about this
apparent gap in communication between

Holz 7

genders? In his article published in
Leadership, Jeffrey Arthurs offers the
obvious suggestion that women should make an
attempt to understand the male model of
communication and that men should make an
attempt to understand the female model of
communication.

However, in his article "Speaking across
the Gender Gap," David Cohen mentions that
experts didn't think it would be helpful to
teach men to communicate more like women and
women to communicate more like men. This
attempt would prove unproductive because it
would go against what men and women have
been taught since birth. Rather than change
the genders to be more like one another, we
could simply try to "understand" each other
better.

In addition, Richard Weaver makes this
observation: "The idea that women should
translate their experiences into the male
code in order to express themselves
effectively . . . is an outmoded,
inconsistent, subservient notion that should
no longer be given credibility in modern
society" (439). He suggests three things we
can change: 1.) Change the norm by which
leadership success is judged, 2.) Redefine
what we mean by power, and 3.) Become more
sensitive to the places and times when
inequity and inequality occur (Weaver 439).
Similarly, Yancey offers advice to help

combat "cross-cultural" fights. He suggests:
1.) Identify your fighting style, 2.) Agree
on rules of engagement, and 3.) Identify the
real issue behind the conflict (Yancey 71).

McCluskey claims men and women need
honest communication that shows respect, and
they must "manage conflict in a way that
maintains the relationship and gets the job
done" (5). She says, "To improve
relationships and interactions between men
and women, we must acknowledge the
differences that do exist, understand how
they develop, and discard dogma about what
are the 'right' roles of women and men" (5).

Obviously, differences exist in the way
men and women communicate, whether caused by
biological and/or environmental factors. We
can consider the possible causes, the
consequences, and possible solutions. Using
this knowledge, we should be able to more
accurately interpret communication between
the genders.

Holz 9

Works Cited

Arthurs, Jeffrey. "He Said, She Heard: Any
Time You Speak to Both Men and Women,
You're Facing Cross-Cultural
Communication." <u>Leadership</u> 23.1
(2002): 49. Expanded Academic Index.
Austin Peay State U., Woodward Lib. 22
Apr 2005 <http://www.galegroup.com/
search>.

Basow, Susan A., and Kimberly Rubenfeld.
"'Troubles Talk': Effects of Gender
and Gender Typing." <u>Sex Roles: A
Journal of Research</u> (2003): 183-87.
Expanded Academic. Austin Peay State
U., Woodward Lib. 24 Apr. 2005 <http://
web5.infotrac.galegroup.com/search>.

Cohen, David. "Speaking across the Gender
Gap." <u>New Scientist</u> 131.1783 (1991):
36. Expanded Academic. Austin Peay
State U, Woodward Lib. 8 Apr 2005.
<http://web5.infotrac.galegroup.com/
search>.

<u>Deborah Tannen & Robert Bly: Men & Women
Talking Together</u>. New York Open
Center. Videocassette. Mystic Fire
Video, 1993.

Glass, Lillian. <u>He Says, She Says: Closing
the Communication Gap between the
Sexes</u>. New York: G.P. Putnam's Sons,
1992.

*The separate
Works Cited
page gives
full
information
on each
source cited
in the paper.*

Holz 10

James, Tammy, and Bethann Cinelli.
   "Exploring Gender-Based Communication
   Styles." <u>Journal of School Health</u> 73
   (2003): 41–42.
McCluskey, Karen Curnow. "Gender at Work."
   <u>Public Management</u> 79.5 (1997): 5–10.
Tannen, Deborah. <u>The Argument Culture:</u>
   <u>Moving from Debate to Dialogue</u>. New
   York: Random House, 1998.
– – –. <u>You Just Don't Understand: Women</u>
   <u>and Men in Conversation</u>. New York:
   Ballantine, 1990.
Warren, Andrea. "How to Get Him to
   Listen." <u>Ladies' Home Journal</u> 113
   (Mar. 1996): 106.
Weaver, Richard L. "Leadership for the
   Future: A New Set of Priorities."
   <u>Vital Speeches of the Day</u> 61 (1995):
   438–41.
Witt, Susan D. "Parental Influence on
   Children's Socialization to Gender
   Roles." <u>Adolescence</u> 32 (1997): 253.
Woods, Julia T. <u>Gendered Lives</u>. San
   Francisco: Wadsworth, 2002.
Yancey, Phillip. "Do Men and Women Speak
   the Same Language?" <u>Marriage</u>
   <u>Partnership</u> 10 (1993): 68–73.

Your Research Project

1. Look carefully at each of the sources you have collected so far—sections of books, journal articles, Internet printouts. Try writing a summary of each one. At the same time, make decisions about material worthy of direct quotation and material that you wish to paraphrase or summarize.

2. Decide how you will keep your notes—in a research journal or in a computer file. Note: the computer files will serve you well because you can transfer them into your text and save typing time.

3. Write various types of notes, that is, write a few that use direct quotations, some that paraphrase, and some that summarize.

4. Conscientiously and with dedication, write as many personal notes as possible. These will be your ideas and they will establish your voice and position. That is, do not let the sources speak for you, let your personal ideas support your position.

5. If you have access to *Take Note!* or some other notetaking program, take the time to consider its special features. You can create notes, store them in folders, and even search your own files by keyword, category, and reference.

CHAPTER EIGHT

DRAFTING THE PAPER IN AN ACADEMIC STYLE

As you draft your paper, you should adopt an academic style that reflects your discipline, as discussed next in section 8a. Present a fair, balanced treatment of the subject. Mentioning opposing viewpoints early in a report gives you something to work against and may strengthen your conclusion. Keep in mind that negative findings have value and should be reported even if they contradict your original hypothesis (see page 113 for more on the logic and ethics of a presentation).

Three principles for drafting may serve your needs:

- *Be practical.* Write portions of the paper when you are ready, skipping over sections of your outline. Leave plenty of space for notes and corrections.
- *Be uninhibited.* Write without fear or delay because initial drafts are attempts to get words on the page rather than to create a polished document.
- *Be conscientious about citations.* Cite the names of the sources in your notes and text, enclose quotations, and preserve page numbers to the sources.

This chapter will help you find the style necessary for your field of study, focus your argument, and build the introduction, body, and conclusion.

8a Writing for Your Field of Study

Each discipline has its own special language, style of expression, and manuscript format. You will, in time, learn fully the style for your college major. Meanwhile, we can identify a few characteristics to guide your writing styles for papers in the humanities.

Academic Style in the Humanities

Writing in one of the humanities requires you to adopt a certain style, as shown in the following example:

> Organ and tissue donation is the gift of life. Each year many people confront health problems due to diseases or congenital birth defects. Tom Taddonia explains that tissues such as skin, veins, and valves can be used to correct congenital defects, blindness, visual impairment, trauma, burns, dental defects, arthritis, cancer, vascular and heart disease.(34) Steve Barnill says, "More than 400 people each month receive the gift of sight through yet another type of tissue donation—corneal transplants. In many cases, donors unsuitable for organ donation are eligible for tissue donation." Barnill notes that tissues are now used in orthopedic surgery, cardiovascular surgery, plastic surgery, dentistry, and podiatry. Even so, not enough people are willing to donate organs and tissues.

Writing in the humanities often displays these characteristics:

- Preoccupation with the quality of life, of art, of ideas (as shown in the first sentence and as echoed in the final sentence)
- Personal involvement on ethical standards
- Use of the present tense to indicate that this problem is an enduring one for humans of past ages as well as the present and the future
- Use of MLA style
- Discussion of theory as supported by the literature

8b Focusing Your Argument

Your writing style in the research paper must be factual, but it should also reflect your thinking on the topic. You will be able to draft your paper more quickly if you focus on the central issue(s). Each paragraph should build on and amplify your primary claim.

Persuading, Inquiring, and Negotiating

Establishing a purpose for writing is one way to focus your argument. Do you wish to persuade, inquire, negotiate? Most research papers make an inquiry.

Persuasion means that you wish to convince the reader that your position is valid and, perhaps, to take action. For example:

> Research has shown that homeowners and wild animals
> cannot live together in harmony. Thus, we need to
> establish green zones in every city of this country
> to control the sprawl in urban areas and to protect
> a segment of the natural habitat for the animals.

Inquiry is an exploratory approach to a problem in which you examine the issues without the insistence of persuasion. It is a truth-seeking adventure. You often must examine, test, or observe in order to discuss the implications of the research. For example:

> Many suburban home dwellers complain that deer,
> raccoons, and other wild animals ravage their
> gardens, flowerbeds, and garbage cans; however, the
> animals were there first. This study will examine
> the problem in one subdivision of 142 homes. How
> have animals been affected by the intrusion of
> human beings? How have homeowners been harassed by
> the animals? The research will examine each side of
> the conflict by interviews will homeowners and
> observation of the animals.

Negotiation is a search for a solution. It means that you attempt to resolve a conflict by inventing options or a mediated solution. For example:

> Suburban neighbors need to find ways to embrace the
> wild animals that have been displaced rather than
> voice anger at the animals or the county
> government. Research has shown that green zones and
> wilderness trails would solve some of the problems;

however, such a solution would require serious
negotiations with real estate developers, who want
to use every square foot of every development.

Maintaining a Focus with Ethical and Logical Appeals

As an objective writer, you will need to examine the problem, make your claim, and provide supporting evidence. Moderation of your voice, even during argument, suggests control of the situation, both emotionally and intellectually. Your voice alerts the audience to your point of view in two ways:

> *Ethical appeal.* If you project the image of one who knows and cares about the topic, the reader will recognize and respect your deep interest in the subject and the way you have carefully crafted your argument. The reader will also appreciate your attention to research conventions.

> *Logical appeal.* For readers to believe in your position, you must provide sufficient evidence in the form of statistical data, paraphrases, and direct quotations from authorities on the subject.

The issue of organ donation, for example, elicits different reactions. Some people argue from the logical position that organs are available and should be used to help people in need. Others argue from the ethical position that organs might be harvested prematurely or that organ donation violates religious principles. As a writer, you must balance your ethical and logical appeals to your readers.

Focusing the Final Thesis Sentence or Hypothesis

Refining your thesis may keep your paper on track. A thesis statement expresses the theory you hope to support with evidence and arguments. A hypothesis is a theory you hope to prove by investigating, testing, and/or observing. Both the thesis and the hypothesis are propositions you want to maintain, analyze, and prove. A final thesis statement or hypothesis will perform three tasks:

1. Establish a claim to control and focus the entire paper.
2. Provide unity and a sense of direction.
3. Specify to the reader the point of the research.

For example, one student started with the topic *exorbitant tuition*, narrowed it to the phrase "tuition fees put parents in debt," and ultimately crafted this thesis:

> The exorbitant tuition at America's colleges is forcing out the poor and promoting an elitist class.

This statement focuses the argument on the effects of high fees on enrollment. The student must prove the assertion by gathering and tabulating statistics.

Questions focus the thesis. If you have trouble finding a claim or argument, ask yourself a few questions. One of the answers might serve as the thesis or the hypothesis.

- What is the point of my research?

  HYPOTHESIS: A delicate balance of medicine, diet, and exercise can control diabetes mellitus.

- Can I tell the reader anything new or different?

  HYPOTHESIS: Most well water in Rutherford county is unsafe for drinking.

- Do I have a solution to the problem?

  THESIS: Public support for "safe" houses will provide a haven for children who are abused by their parents.

- Do I have a new slant and new approach to the issue?

  HYPOTHESIS: Poverty, not greed, forces many youngsters into a life of crime.

- Should I take the minority view of this matter?

  THESIS: Give credit where it is due: Custer may have lost the battle at Little Bighorn, but Crazy Horse and his men, with inspiration from Sitting Bull, won the battle.

- Will an enthymeme serve my purpose by making a claim in a *because* clause?

ENTHYMEME: Sufficient organ and tissue donation,
enough to satisfy the demand, remains
almost impossible because negative myths
and religious concerns dominate the
minds of many people.

CHECKLIST WRITING THE FINAL THESIS

You should be able to answer *yes* to each question below:

- Does the thesis express your position in a full, declarative statement that is not a question, not a statement of purpose, and not merely a topic?

- Does it limit the subject to a narrow focus that grows out of research?

- Does it establish an investigation, interpretation, or theoretical presentation?

- Does it point forward to your findings and a discussion of the implications in your conclusion?

Key words focus the thesis or the hypothesis. Use the important words from your notes and rough outline to refine your thesis sentence. For example, during your reading of several novels or short stories by Flannery O'Connor, you might have jotted down certain repetitions of image, theme, or character. The key words might be *death, ironic moments of humor, hysteria and passion, human shortcomings,* or other issues that O'Connor repeatedly explored. These concrete ideas might point you toward a general thesis:

The tragic endings of Flannery O'Connor's stories
depict desperate people coming face to face with
their own shortcomings.

Change your thesis but not your hypothesis. Be willing to abandon your preliminary thesis if research leads you to new and different issues. However, a hypothesis *cannot* be adjusted or changed. It will be proved true, partially true, or untrue. Your negative findings have value, for you will have disproved the hypothesis so others need not duplicate your research. For example, the hypothesis might assert: "Industrial pollution is seeping into water tables and traveling many miles into neighboring well water of Lamar county." Your report may prove the truth of the hypothesis, but it may not. It may only establish a probability and the need for additional research.

8c Designing an Academic Title

A clearly expressed title, like a good thesis sentence, will focus your writing and keep you on course. Although writing a final title may not be feasible until the paper is written, a preliminary title can provide specific words of identification to help you stay focused. For example, one writer began with this title: "Diabetes." Then, to be more specific, the writer added another word: "Diabetes Management." As research developed and she recognized the role of medicine, diet, and exercise for victims, she refined the title even more: "Diabetes Management: A Delicate Balance of Medicine, Diet, and Exercise." Thereby, she and her readers had a clear idea that the paper was about three methods of managing the disease.

Long titles are standard in scholarly writing. Consider the following examples:

1. Subject, colon, and focusing phrase:

   Organ and Tissue Donation and Transplantation:
   Myths, Ethical Issues, and Lives Saved

2. Subject, focusing prepositional phrase:

   Prayer at School-Related Activities

3. Subject, colon, type of study:

   Black Dialect in Maya Angelou's Poetry: A Language
   Study

4. Subject, colon, focusing question:

   AIDS: Where Did It Come From?

5. Subject, comparative study:

   Religious Imagery in N. Scott Momaday's <u>The Names</u>
   and Heronimous Storm's <u>Seven Arrows</u>

8d Drafting the Paper

As you begin drafting your research report, work systematically through a preliminary plan or outline to keep order as your notes expand your research (see pages 63–71 for models of organization). Use your notes, photocopies, downloaded material, and research journal to transfer materials directly into the text, remembering always to provide citations to borrowed information. Do not quote an entire paragraph unless it is crucial to your discussion and cannot be easily reduced to a summary. In addition, be conscious of basic writing conventions, as described next.

Writing with Unity and Coherence

Unity refers to exploring one topic in depth to give your writing a single vision. With unity, each paragraph carefully expands on a single aspect of the narrowed subject. *Coherence* connects the parts logically by:

* repetition of key words and sentence structures
* the judicious use of pronouns and synonyms
* the effective placement of transitional words and phrases (e.g., *also, furthermore, therefore, in addition,* and *thus)*

Writing in the Proper Tense

Verb tense often distinguishes a paper in the humanities from one in the natural and social sciences. While the social sciences and the physical sciences employ past tense, use the present tense in the humanities. MLA style employs the present tense to cite an author's work (e.g., "Patel *explains"* or "the work of Scoggin and Roberts *shows").* The ideas and the words of the writers remain in print and continue to be true in the universal present. Therefore, when writing a paper in the humanities, use the historical present tense, as shown here:

"It was the best of times, it was the worst of times," writes Charles Dickens about the eighteenth century.

Johnson argues that sociologist Norman Wayman has a "narrow-minded view of clerics and their role in the community" (64).

Using the Language of the Discipline

Every discipline and every topic has its own vocabulary. Therefore, while reading and taking notes, jot down words and phrases relevant to your research study. Get comfortable with them so you can use them effectively. For example, a child abuse topic requires the language of sociology and psychology, thereby demanding an acquaintance with the following terms:

social worker	maltreatment	aggressive behavior
poverty levels	guardians	incestuous relations
stress	hostility	battered child
formative years	recurrence	behavioral patterns

Many writers create a terminology list to strengthen their command of appropriate nouns and verbs for the subject in question.

Using Source Material to Enhance Your Writing

Readers want to see your thoughts and ideas on a subject. For this reason, a paragraph should seldom contain source material only; it must contain a topic sentence to establish a point for the research evidence. Every paragraph should explain, analyze, and support a thesis, not merely string together a set of quotations. The following passage effectively cites two sources.

> Two factors that have played a part in farm land
> becoming drought prone are "light, sandy soil and
> soils with high alkalinity" (Boughman 234). In
> response, Bjornson says that drought resistant
> plants exist along parts of the Mediterranean Sea.
> Thus, hybrids of these plants may serve Texas
> farmers (34).

The short passage weaves the sources effectively into a whole, uses the sources as a natural extension of the discussion, and cites each source separately and appropriately.

Writing in the Third Person

Write your paper with third-person narration that avoids "I believe" or "It is my opinion." Rather than saying, "I think television violence affects children," drop the opening two words and say, "Television violence affects

children." Readers will understand that the statement is your thought
and one that you will defend with evidence.

Writing with the Passive Voice in an Appropriate Manner

The passive voice is often less forceful than an active verb. However,
research writers sometimes need to use the passive voice verb, as shown
here:

    Forty-three students of a third-grade class at
    Barksdale School were observed for two weeks.

This usage of the passive voice is fairly standard in the social sciences
and the natural or applied sciences. The passive voice is preferred because
it keeps the focus on the subject of the research, not the writer (you would
not want to say, "I observed the students").

Placing Graphics Effectively in a Research Essay

Use graphics to support your text. Most computers allow you to create tables, line graphs, and pie charts as well as diagrams, maps, and
original designs. You may also import tables and illustrations from
your sources. Place these graphics as close as possible to the parts
of the text to which they relate. It is acceptable to use full-color art
if your printer prints in color; however, use black for the captions and
date. Place a full-page graphic on a separate sheet after making a
textual reference to it (e.g., "see Table 7"). Place graphics in an
appendix when you have several complex items that might distract the
reader from your textual message. See page 249 in the Appendix for
help with designing tables, line graphs, illustrations, pie charts, and
other visuals.

Avoiding Sexist and Biased Language

The best writers exercise caution against words that may stereotype any
person, regardless of gender, race, nationality, creed, age, or disability.
The following are guidelines to help you avoid discriminatory language:

Age. Review the accuracy of your statement. It is appropriate to use
boy and *girl* for children of high school age and under. *Young man* and
young woman or *male adolescent* and *female adolescent* can be appropriate, but *teenager* carries a certain bias. Avoid *elderly* as a noun; use
older persons.

Gender. *Gender* is a term used culturally to identify men and women within their social groups. *Sex* tends to refer to a biological factor (see below for a discussion of sexual orientation).

- Use plural subjects so that nonspecific, plural pronouns are grammatically correct. For example, you may specify that Judy Jones maintains *her* lab equipment in sterile condition or indicate that technicians, in general, maintain *their* own equipment.
- Reword the sentence so a pronoun is unnecessary, as in *The doctor prepared the necessary surgical equipment without interference.*
- Use pronouns that denote gender only when necessary when gender has been previously established, as in *Mary, as a new laboratory technician, must learn to maintain her equipment in sterile condition.*
- The use of *woman* and *female* as adjectives varies. Use *woman* or *women* in most instances (e.g., *a woman's intuition)* and use *female* for species and statistics, (e.g., *four female subjects).* Avoid the use of *lady,* as in *lady pilot.*
- The first mention of a person requires the full name (e.g., Ernest Hemingway, Joan Didion) and thereafter requires the use of the surname only (e.g., Hemingway, Didion). In general, avoid formal titles (e.g., Dr., Gen., Mrs., Ms., Lt., Prof.). Avoid their equivalents in other languages (e.g., Mme, Dame, Monsieur).
- Avoid *man and wife* or *7 men and 16 females.* Keep terms parallel by matching *husband and wife* or *man and woman* and *7 male rats and 16 female rats.*

Sexual Orientation. The term *sexual orientation* is preferred to the term *sexual preference.* It is preferable to use *lesbians* and *gay men* rather than *homosexuals.* The terms *heterosexual, homosexual,* and *bisexual* can be used to describe both the identity and the behavior of subjects—that is, as adjectives.

Ethnic and Racial Identity. Some persons prefer the term *Black,* others prefer *African-American,* and still others prefer *a person of color.* The terms *Negro* and *Afro-American* are now dated and not appropriate. Use *Black* and *White,* not the lowercase *black* and *white.* In like manner, some individuals may prefer *Hispanic* or *Latino.* Use the term *Asian* or *Asian American* rather than *Oriental.* *Native American* is a broad term that includes *Samoans, Hawaiians,* and *American Indians.* A good rule of thumb is to use a person's nationality when it is known (*Mexican, Canadian, Comanche,* or *Nigerian*).

Disability. In general, place people first, not their disability. Rather than *disabled person* or *retarded child* say *person who has scoliosis* or *a child with Down syndrome.* Avoid saying *a challenged person* or *a special child* in favor of *a person with* or *a child with.* Remember that a *disability* is a physical quality while a *handicap* is a limitation that might be imposed by nonphysical factors, such as stairs or poverty or social attitudes.

8e Creating an Introduction, Body, and Conclusion

Writing the Introduction

Use the first few paragraphs of your paper to establish the nature of your study.

SUBJECT: Does your introduction identify your specific topic, and then define, limit, and narrow it to one issue?

BACKGROUND: Does your introduction provide relevant historical data or discuss a few key sources that touch on your specific issue?

PROBLEM: Does your introduction identify a problem and explain the complications your research paper will explore or resolve?

THESIS: Does your introduction use your thesis sentence or hypothesis within the first few paragraphs to establish the direction of the study and to point your readers toward your eventual conclusions?

How you work these essential elements into the beginning of your paper depends on your style of writing. They need not appear in this order, nor should you cram all these items into a short, opening paragraph. Feel free to write a long introduction by using more than one of these techniques:

Open with your thesis statement or hypothesis.

Open with a quotation.

Relate your topic to the well known.

Provide background information.

Review the literature.

Provide a brief summary.

Define key terms.

Supply data, statistics, and special evidence.

Take exception to critical views.

Use an anecdote as a hook to draw your reader into the essay.

The following sample of an introduction gives background information, establishes a persuasive position, reviews key literature, takes exception, gives key terms, and offers a thesis.

> John Berendt's popular and successful novel
> <u>Midnight in the Garden of Good and Evil</u> skillfully
> presents the unpredictable twists and turns of a
> landmark murder case set under the moss-hung live
> oaks of Savannah, Georgia. While it is written as a
> novel, the nonfiction account of this tragic murder
> case reveals the intriguing and sometimes deranged
> relationships that thrive in a town where everyone
> knows everyone else. However, the mystique of the
> novel does not lie with the murder case but with
> the collection of unusual and often complex
> characters, including a voodoo priestess, a young
> southern gigolo, and a black drag queen (e.g.,
> Bilkin, Miller, and especially Carson, who
> describes the people of Savannah as "a type of
> Greek chorus" [14]). Berendt's success lies in his
> carefully crafted characterization.

Writing the Body of the Research Paper

When writing the body, you should keep in mind three elements:

ANALYSIS: Classify the major issues of the study and provide a careful analysis of each in defense of your thesis.

PRESENTATION:	Provide well-reasoned statements at the beginning of your paragraphs and supply evidence of support with proper documentation.
PARAGRAPHS:	Offer a variety of paragraphs to compare, show process, narrate the history of the subject, and show causes.

Use these techniques to build substantive paragraphs for your paper:

Relate a time sequence.

Compare or contrast issues, the views of experts, and nature of literary characters.

Develop cause and effect.

Issue a call to action.

Define key terminology.

Show a process.

Ask questions and provide answers.

Cite evidence from source materials.

Explain the methods used and the design of the study.

Present the results of the investigation with data, statistics, and graphics.

The following paragraph idemonstrates the use of several techniques—an overview of the problem, citing a source, comparing issues, cause and effect, key terms, and process.

To burn or not to burn the natural forests in the national parks is the question. The pyrophobic public voices its protests while environmentalists praise the rejuvenating effects of a good forest fire. It is difficult to convince people that not all fire is bad. The public has visions of Smokey the Bear campaigns and mental images of Bambi and Thumper fleeing the roaring flames. Chris Bolgiano explains that federal policy evolved slowly "from the basic impulse to douse all fires immediately to a sophisticated decision matrix based on the functions of any given unit of land" (23). Bolgiano declares that "timber production, grazing, recreation, and wilderness preservation elicit different fire-management approaches" (23).

Writing the Conclusion of the Paper

The conclusion is not a summary; it is a discussion of beliefs and findings based on your reasoning and on the evidence and results you presented. Select appropriate items from this list.

THESIS:	Reaffirm the thesis sentence, the hypothesis, or the central mission of your study. If appropriate, give a statement in support or nonsupport of an original enthymeme or hypothesis.
JUDGMENT:	Discuss and interpret the findings. Give answers. Now is the time to draw inferences, emphasize a theory, and find relevance in the results.
DIRECTIVES:	Based on the theoretical implications of the study, offer suggestions for action and for new research.
DISCUSSION:	Discuss the implications of your findings from testing or observation.

Use these techniques to write the conclusion:

Restate the thesis and reach beyond it.

Close with an effective quotation.

Return the focus of a literary study to the author.

Compare the past to the present.

Offer a directive or a solution.

Give a call to action.

Discuss the implications of your findings.

The following example of a conclusion provides an interpretation of the results of an experiment as well as the implications of the results.

The results of this experiment were similar to expectations, but perhaps the statistical significance, because of the small subject size, was biased toward the delayed conditions of the curve. Barker and Peay have addressed this point. The subjects were not truly representative of the total population because of their prior exposure to test procedures. Another factor that may have affected the curves was the presentation of the data. The images on the screen were available for five seconds, and that amount of time may have enabled the subjects to store each image effectively. If the time period for each image were reduced to one or two seconds, there could be lower recall scores, thereby reducing the differences between the control group and the experimental group.

8f   Revising the Rough Draft

Once you have the complete paper in a rough draft, the serious business of editing begins. First, you should revise your paper on a global scale, moving blocks of material around to the best advantage and into the proper format. Second, edit the draft with a line-by-line examination of wording and technical excellence. Third, proofread the final version to assure that your words are spelled correctly and the text is grammatically sound.

Revision can turn a passable paper into an excellent one. Revise the manuscript on a global scale by looking at its overall design. Do the introduction, body, and conclusion have substance? Do the paragraphs maintain the flow of your central proposition? Does the paper fulfill the requirements of the academic model?

Editing Before Printing the Final Manuscript

Global revision is complemented by careful editing of paragraphs, sentences, and individual words. Travel through the paper to study your citation of the sources. Confirm that you have properly quoted or paraphrased each cited source. Check spelling with both the computer and your own visual examination. Here are eight additional tasks:

1. Cut phrases and sentences that do not advance your main ideas or that merely repeat what your sources have already stated.

2. Determine that coordinated, balanced ideas are appropriately expressed and that minor ideas are properly subordinated.

3. Change most of your *to be* verbs (is, are, was) to stronger active verbs.

4. Maintain the present tense in most verbs.

5. Convert passive structures to active unless you want to emphasize the subject, not the actor (see page 117).

6. Confirm that you have introduced paraphrases and quotations so they flow smoothly into your text.

7. Use formal, academic style, and be on guard against clusters of little monosyllabic words that fail to advance ideas. Examine your wording for its effectiveness in the context of your subject (see page 118).

8. Examine your paragraphs for transitions that move the reader effectively from one paragraph to the next.

Using the Computer to Edit Your Text

Some software programs examine your grammar and mechanics, look for parentheses that you opened but never closed, find unpaired quotation marks, flag passive verbs, question your spelling, and mark other items for your correction. Pay attention to the caution flags raised by this type of program. After a software program examines the style of your manuscript, you should revise and edit the text to improve stylistic weaknesses. Remember, it is your paper, not the computer's.

Participating in Peer Review

Peer review has two sides. First, it means handing your paper to a friend or classmate, asking for opinions and suggestions. Second, it means reviewing a classmate's research paper. You can learn by reviewing as well as by writing. Your instructor may supply a peer review sheet, or you can use the accompanying checklist. Criticize the paper constructively on each point.

CHECKLIST PEER REVIEW

1. Are the subject and the accompanying issues introduced early?

2. Is the writer's critical approach to the problem stated clearly in a thesis sentence? Is it placed effectively in the introduction?

3. Do the paragraphs of the body have individual unity—that is, does each paragraph develop an important idea and only one idea? Does each paragraph relate to the thesis?

4. Are sources introduced, usually with the name of the expert, and then cited by a page number in parentheses? Keep in mind that Internet sources rarely have page numbers.

5. Is it clear where a paraphrase begins and where it ends?

6. Are the sources relevant to the argument?

Proofreading

Print a hard copy of your manuscript. Proofread this final version with great care.

CHECKLIST PROOFREADING

1. Check for errors in sentence structure, spelling, and punctuation.

2. Check for hyphenation and word division. Remember that no words should be hyphenated at the ends of lines.

3. Read each quotation for accuracy of your own wording and of the words within your quoted materials. Check for opening and closing quotation marks.

4. Doublecheck intext citations to be certain that each one is correct and that each source is listed on your Works Cited page at the end of the paper.

5. Doublecheck the format—the title page, margins, spacing, content notes, and many other elements.

Your Research Project

1. Examine your own thesis using the Final Thesis Checklist on page 115. Revise your thesis as necessary.

2. Write an academic title for your paper, one that clearly describes the nature of your work (see page 116).

3. After you draft a significant portion of the paper, review it carefully for each of these items: coherence, proper tense, third person voice, and the language of the discipline.

CHAPTER NINE

UNDERSTANDING AND AVOIDING PLAGIARISM

This chapter defines plagiarism, explores the ethical standards for writing in an academic environment, and provides examples of the worst and best of citations. Plus, we must face the newest problem: The Internet makes it easy to copy and download material and paste it into a paper—which in itself is not a problem *unless* you fail to acknowledge the source.

Intellectual property has value. If you write a song, you have a right to protect your interests. Thus, the purpose of this chapter is to explore with you the ethics of research writing, especially about these matters:

- Using sources to enhance your credibility
- Using sources to place a citation in its proper context
- Honoring property rights
- Avoiding plagiarism
- Honoring and crediting sources in online course work

9a Using Sources to Enhance Your Credibility

What some students fail to realize is that citing a source in their papers, even the short ones, signals something special and positive to readers—that the student has researched the topic, explored the literature about it, and has the expertise to share it. By announcing clearly the name of a source, the writer reveals the scope of his or her critical reading in the literature, as shown in these notes by one student:

> Sandra Postel says water is "a living system that drives the workings of a natural world we depend on" (19). Postel declares: "A new water era has begun" (24). She indicates that the great prairies of the world will dry up, including America's. Hey, when folks in America notice the drought, then maybe something will happen. Let's watch what happens when Texas goes dry as a bone.

These notes give clear evidence of the writer's investigation into the subject, and they enhance the student's image as a researcher. This student will receive credit for naming and quoting the source. The opposite, *plagiarism*, might get the student into trouble, as we discuss in section 9d.

9b Identifying Bias in a Source

You will show integrity in your use of sources by identifying any bias expressed by a writer or implied by the political stance of a magazine. For example, if you are writing about federal aid to farmers, you will find different opinions in a farmer's magazine and a journal that promotes itself as a watchdog to federal spending. One is an advocate and the other a vocal opponent. You may quote these sources, but only if you identify them carefully. Let us examine the problem faced by one student. Norman Berkowitz, in researching articles on the world's water supply, found an article of interest but positioned it with a description of the source, as shown in this note that carefully identifies the source of an alarmist attitude.

> Earth First, which describes itself as a radical environmental journal, features articles by an editorial staff that uses pseudonyms, such as Sky, Jade, Wedge, and Sprig. In the article "The End of Lake Powell," Sprig says, "The Colorado River may soon be unable to provide for the 25 million people plumbed into its system" (25). The danger, however,

```
is not limited to Lake Powell. Sprig adds, "This
overconsumption of water, compounded with a
regional drought cycle of 15 years, could mean that
Lake Power and every other reservoir in the upper
Colorado River area will be without water" (24-25).
```

You owe your readers this favor: Examine articles, especially those in magazines and on the Internet, for special interests, opinionated speculation, or an absence of credentials by the writer. Be wary of Web sites without an academic or government sponsor. Refer to Chapter 2, which lists the most reliable databases.

9c Honoring Property Rights

If you invent a new piece of equipment or a child's toy, you can get a patent that protects your invention. You now own it. If you own a company, you can register a symbol that serves as a trademark for the products produced. You own the trademark. In like manner, if you write a set of poems and publish them in a chapbook, you own the poems. Others must seek your permission before they can reproduce the poems, just as others must buy your trademark or pay to produce your toy.

The principle behind the copyright law is relatively simple. Copyright begins at the time a creative work is recorded in some tangible form— a written document, a drawing, a tape recording. It does not depend on a legal registration with the copyright office in Washington, DC, although published works are usually registered. The moment you express yourself creatively on paper, in a song, on a canvas, that expression is your intellectual property. You have a vested interest in any profits made from the distribution of your work. For that reason, songwriters, cartoonists, fiction writers, and other artists guard their work and do not want it disseminated without compensation.

Scholarly work rarely involves direct compensation, but recognition is certainly an important need. We provide recognition by means of in-text citations and bibliography entries. As a student, you may use copyrighted material in your research paper under a doctrine of *fair use* as described in the U.S. Code, which says:

> The fair use of a copyrighted work . . . for purposes such as criticism, comment, news reporting, teaching (including multiple copies for classroom use), scholarship, or research is not an infringement of copyright.

Thus, as long as you borrow for educational purposes, such as a paper to be read by your instructor, you should not be concerned about violating the copyright law, as long as you provide documentation. However, if you decide to *publish* your research paper on a Web site, then new considerations come into play and you should seek the advice of your instructor.

9d Avoiding Plagiarism

Write most of the paper yourself. First, develop personal notes full of your own ideas on a topic. Discover how you feel about the issue. Then, rather than copying sources one after another, express your own ideas at the beginning of paragraphs and then synthesize the ideas of others by using summary, paraphrase, and quotation. Rethink and reconsider ideas you gathered in your reading, make meaningful connections, and, when you refer to a specific source—as you inevitably will—give it credit.

Plagiarism is offering the words or ideas of another person as one's own. Major violations, which can bring failure in the course or expulsion from school, are:

- The use of another student's work
- The purchase of a canned research paper
- Copying passages into your paper without documentation
- Copying a key, well-worded phrase without documentation
- Placing specific ideas of others in your own words without documentation

These instances represent deliberate attempts to deceive. Closely related, but not technically plagiarism, is the fabrication of information—that is, making information up off the top of your head. Some newspaper reporters have lost their jobs because of such fabrication.

A gray area in plagiarism is simply student carelessness—for example, failure to enclose quoted material within quotation marks even though you provide an in-text citation, or a paraphrase that never quite becomes paraphrase because too much of the original is left intact. In this area, instructors might step in and help the beginning researcher, for although these cases are not flagrant instances of plagiarism, such errors can mar an otherwise fine piece of research.

There is one safety net: Express clearly the name of your sources to let readers know the scope of your reading on the subject, as in this note:

```
Commenting on the role that music has in our
everyday lives, editor Marc Smirnoff makes this
observation in Oxford American: "The music that
human beings rely on is essential to them. We know
which tunes to listen to when we need an all-
important lift (or when the party does) or when we
want to wallow in our sadness. (4)
```

Citations like the one above help establish your credibility because they make clear whom you have read and how your ideas blend with the source.

CHECKLIST DOCUMENTING YOUR SOURCES

- Let a reader know when you begin borrowing from a source by introducing a quotation or paraphrase with the name of the authority.
- Enclose within quotation marks all quoted materials—keywords, phrases, sentences, paragraphs.
- Make certain that paraphrased material is rewritten in your own style and language. The simple rearrangement of sentence patterns is unacceptable.
- Provide specific in-text documentation for each borrowed item, but keep in mind that styles differ for MLA, APA, CSE, and CMS standards. These styles are explained in later chapters.
- Provide a bibliography entry on the Works Cited page for every source cited in the paper.

Common Knowledge Exceptions

Common knowledge exceptions exist because you and your reader share some perspectives on a subject. For example, if you attend the University of Delaware, you need not cite the fact that Wilmington is the state's largest city, or that Dover is the capital city. Information of this sort requires *no* in-text citation because your local audience will be knowledgeable.

> The extended shoreline of Delaware provides one of
> the most extensive series of national wildlife
> refuges in the eastern United States. The state
> stretches from its northern border with
> Philadelphia to form a 100-mile border with
> Maryland to its west and south. Its political
> center is Dover, in the center of the state, but
> its commercial center is Wilmington, a great
> industrial city situated on Delaware Bay just below
> Philadelphia.

However, a writer in another place and time might need to cite the source of this information. Most writers would probably want to document this next passage.

> Early Indian tribes on the plains called themselves
> *Illiniwek* (which meant "strong men"), and French
> settlers pronounced the name *Illinois* (Angle 44).

Borrowing from a Source Correctly

The next examples in MLA style demonstrate the differences between the accurate use of a source and the dark shades of plagiarism. First is the original reference material; it is followed by several student versions, with discussions of their merits.

Original Material

Imagine your brain as a house filled with lights. Now imagine someone turning off the lights one by one. That's what Alzheimer's disease does. It turns off the lights so that the flow of ideas, emotions and memories from one room to the next slows and eventually ceases. And sadly—as anyone who has ever watched a parent, a sibling, a spouse succumb to the spreading darkness knows—there is no way to stop the lights from turning off, no way to switch them back on once they've grown dim. At least not yet.

But sooner than one might have dared hope, predicts Harvard University neurologist Dr. Dennis Selkoe, Alzheimer's disease will shed the veneer of invincibility that today makes it such a terrifying affliction. Medical practitioners, he believes, will shortly have on hand not one but several drugs capable of slowing—and perhaps even halting—the progression of the disease. Best of all, a better understanding of genetic and environmental risk factors will lead to much earlier diagnosis, so that patients will receive treatment long before their brains start to fade.

> *From J. Madeleine Nash, "The New Science of Alzheimer's,"*
> Time *17 July 2000: 51.*

Student Version A (Needs Revision)

```
Alzheimer's disease is like having a brain that's
similar to a house filled with lights, but somebody
goes through the house and turns out the lights one
by one until the brain, like the house, is dark.
```

This sentence sounds good, and the reader will probably think so also. However, the writer has borrowed the analogy and much of the wording from the original source, so it's not the student's work. In addition, the writer has provided no documentation whatsoever, nor has the writer named the authority. In truth, the writer implies to the reader that these sentences are an original creation when, actually, nothing belongs to the writer.

Student Version B (Needs Revision)

```
Alzheimer's is a terrifying disease, for both
victim and relatives. However, sooner than we might
expect, medical scientists will have available
several drugs capable of slowing—and perhaps even
halting—the progress of the disease. In addition,
earlier diagnosis will mean patients can receive
treatment before their brains start to go dark.
```

This version borrows keywords from the original without the use of quotation marks and without a citation. The next version provides a citation, but it too has errors.

Student Version C (Needs Minor Revision)

```
Alzheimer's is a terrifying disease, but help is on
the way. Dr. Dennis Selkoe, a neurologist at
Harvard University, predicts that medical
```

practitioners will shortly have on hand several
drugs that will slow or stop the progression of the
disease (Nash 51).

This version is better. It provides a reference to Dr. Selkoe, who has
been cited by Nash. But readers cannot know that the paraphrase contains far too much of Nash's language—words that should be enclosed
within quotation marks. Also, the citation to Nash is ambiguous. The
next version handles these matters in a better fashion.

Student Version D (Acceptable)

Alzheimer's is a terrifying disease, but help is on
the way. In a recent report in *Time*, medical
reporter Madeleine Nash cites Dr. Dennis Selkoe, a
neurologist at Harvard University, who believes
that "medical practitioners . . . will shortly have
on hand not one but several drugs capable of
slowing—and perhaps even halting—the progression of
the disease" (Nash 51).

This version represents a satisfactory handling of the source material. The writer is acknowledged at the outset of the borrowing, the neurologist is given credit for his ideas, and a key section is quoted. A correct
page citation closes the material. Let's suppose, however, that the writer
does not wish to quote directly at all. The following example shows a
paraphrased version:

Student Version E (Acceptable)

Alzheimer's is a terrifying disease, but help is on
the way. In a recent report in *Time*, medical
reporter Madeleine Nash cites Dr. Dennis Selkoe, a
neurologist at Harvard University, who believes
that the scientific community is knocking on the
door of a cure or maybe even a set of cures. The
goal, according to Nash, is to halt the disease or
at least slow its insidious stalking of some of our
best and brightest, such as former President Ronald
Reagan (Nash 51).

This version also represents a satisfactory handling of the source material. In this case, no direct quotation is employed, the author and the authority are acknowledged and credited, and the entire paragraph is paraphrased in the student's own language. *Note:* the reference to the former president is not mentioned in the original passage, but such usage is a prime example of common knowledge (see pages 132–133).

CHECKLIST REQUIRED INSTANCES FOR CITING A SOURCE

1. An original idea derived from a source, whether quoted or para-phrased.

   ```
   Genetic engineering, by which a child's body
   shape and intellectual ability is
   predetermined, raised for one source "memories
   of Nazi attempts in eugenics" (Riddell 19).
   ```

2. Your summary of original ideas by a source.

   ```
   Genetic engineering has been described as the
   rearrangement of the genetic structure in
   animals or in plants, which is a technique that
   takes a section of DNA and reattaches it to
   another section (Rosenthal 19-20).
   ```

3. Factual information that is not common knowledge within the context of the course.

   ```
   Madigan has shown that genetic engineering has
   its risks: a nonpathogenic organism might be
   converted into a pathogenic one or an
   undesirable trait might develop as a result of
   a mistake (15).
   ```

4. Any exact wording copied from a source.

   ```
   Woodward asserted that genetic engineering is
   "a high-stakes moral rumble that involves
   billions of dollars and affects the future"
   (68).
   ```

9e Seeking Permission to Publish Material on Your Web Site

You may wish to include your research papers on your personal Web site, if you have one. However, the moment you do so, you are *publishing* the work and putting it into the public domain. That act carries responsibilities. In particular, the *fair use* doctrine of the U.S. Code refers to the personal educational purposes of your usage. When you load borrowed images, text, music, or artwork onto the Internet, you are making that intellectual property available to everybody all over the world.

Short quotations, a few graphics, and a small quantity of illustrations to support your argument are examples of fair use. Permission is needed, however, if the amount you borrow is substantial. The borrowing cannot affect the market for the original work, and you cannot misrepresent it in any way. The courts are still refining the law. For example, would your use of three *Doonesbury* comic strips be substantial? Yes, if you reproduce them in full. Would it affect the market for the comic strip? Perhaps. Follow these guidelines:

- Seek permission to include copyrighted material you publish within your Web article. Most authors grant permission at no charge. The problem is tracking down the copyright holder.

- If you attempt to get permission and if your motive for using the material is *not for profit*, it's unlikely you will have any problem with the copyright owner. The owner would have to prove that your use of the image or text caused him or her financial harm.

- You may publish without permission works that are in the public domain, such a section of Hawthorne's *The Scarlet Letter* or a speech by the President from the White House. In general, creative works enter the public domain after about seventy-five years (the laws keep changing). Government papers are public domain.

- Document any and all sources you feature on your Web site.

- You may need permission to provide hypertext links to other sites. However, right now the Internet rules on access are being freely interpreted.

- Be prepared for other persons to visit your Web site and even borrow from it. Decide beforehand how you will handle requests for use of your work, especially if it includes your creative efforts in poetry, art, music, or graphic design.

> ■ **HINT:** For information on the Fair Use Laws, visit **http://fairuse.stanford.edu/**.

Your Research Project

1. Begin now to maintain a systematic scrutiny of what you borrow from the sources. Remember that direct quotation reflects the voices of your sources and that paraphrase maintains your voice. Just be certain with paraphrase that you do not borrow the exact wording of the original.

2. Look at your college bulletin and the student handbook. Do they say anything about plagiarism? Do they address the matter of copyright protection?

3. Consult with your writing instructor whenever you have a question about your use of a source. Writing instructors are there to serve you and help you avoid plagiarism.

4. If you think you might publish your paper on the Web and if it contains substantial borrowing from a source, such as five or six cartoons from the *New Yorker* magazine, begin now to seek permission for reproducing the material. In your letter or e-mail, give your name, school, the subject of your research paper, the material you want to borrow, and how you will use it. You may copy or attach the page(s) of your paper in which the material appears.

CHAPTER TEN

BLENDING REFERENCE MATERIAL INTO YOUR WRITING

This chapter explains the MLA style, as established by the Modern Language Association. Used primarily for research projects in composition, literature, English usage, and foreign languages, MLA style asks for the full name of the scholar on first mention but asks only for the last name thereafter and in parenthetical citations.

10a Blending Reference Citations into Your Text

As you might expect, writing a research paper carries with it certain obligations. You should gather scholarly material on the topic and display it prominently in your writing. In addition, you should identify each source used with the authority's name or the title of the work with a page number, except for unprinted sources and most Internet sources. As a general policy, keep citations brief. Remember, your readers will have full documentation to each source on the "Works Cited" page (see Chapter 11).

Making a General Reference without a Page Number

Some references do not require parenthetical citation.

> The women of Thomas Hardy's novels are the special focus of three essays by Nancy Norris, Judith Mitchell, and James Scott.

Beginning with the Author and Ending with a Page Number

Introduce a quotation or a paraphrase with the author's name and close it with a page number, placed inside the parentheses. Try always to use this standard citation because it informs the reader of the beginning and the end of borrowed materials, as shown here:

> Herbert Norfleet states that the use of video games by children improves their hand and eye coordination (45).

In the following example, the reader can easily trace the origin of the ideas.

> Video games for children have opponents and advocates. Herbert Norfleet defends the use of video games by children. He says it improves their hand and eye coordination and that it exercises their minds as they work their way through various puzzles and barriers. Norfleet states, "The mental gymnastics of video games and the competition with fellow players are important to young children for their physical, social, and mental development" (45). Yet some authorities disagree with Norfleet for several reasons.

Putting the Page Number Immediately after the Name

Sometimes, notes at the end of a quotation make it expeditious to place the page number immediately after the name.

> Boughman (46) urges car makers to "direct the force of automotive airbags upward against the windshield" (emphasis added).

Putting the Name and Page Number at the End of Borrowed Material

You can, if you like, put cited names with the page number at the end of a quotation or paraphrase.

"Each DNA strand provides the pattern of bases for
a new strand to form, resulting in two complete
molecules" (Justice, Moody, and Graves 462).

In the case of a paraphrase, you should give your reader a signal to
show when the borrowing begins, as shown next:

One source explains that the DNA in the chromosomes
must be copied perfectly during cell reproduction
(Justice, Moody, and Graves 462).

Use last names only within the parenthetical citation *unless your list
contains more than one author with same last name*, in which case you
should add the author's first initial—"(H. Norfleet 45)" and "(W. Norfleet 432)." If the first initial is also shared, use the full first name "(Her-
bert Norfleet 45)."

> ■ **NOTE:** In MLA style, do not place a comma between the
> name and the page number.

10b Citing a Source When No Author Is Listed

When no author is shown on a title page, cite the title of an article, the
name of the magazine, the name of a bulletin or book, or the name of the
publishing organization. You should abbreviate or use an acronym (e.g.,
BBC or NASA).

> ■ **NOTE:** Search for the author's name at the bottom of the
> opening page, at the end of the article, at an Internet home
> page, or an e-mail address.

Citing the Title of a Magazine Article
Use a shorted version of the title when no author is listed:

The preservation of our natural world, including
green space, mountain ranges, and the seas, can

only be protected with a conscious effort from all
citizens. Conservation efforts are our last resort.
According to a recent article in Audubon magazine,
"Our world may be getting smaller, but roads less
traveled still exist" ("To the Ends").

The Works Cited entry would read:

"To the Ends of the Earth." Audubon July-August
2005: 45.

Citing the Title of a Report

One bank showed a significant decline in assets
despite an increase in its number of depositors
(Annual Report, 2006, 23).

Citing the Name of a Publisher or a Corporate Body

The report by the Clarion County School Board
endorsed the use of Channel One in the school
system and said that "students will benefit by the
news reports more than they will be adversely
affected by advertising" (CCSB 3-4).

10c Citing Nonprint Sources That Have No Page Number

On occasion you may need to identify unprinted sources, such as a
speech, the song lyrics from a compact disk, an interview, or a television program. Since no page number exists, omit the parenthetical citation. Instead, introduce the type of source—for example, lecture, letter,
interview—so that readers do not expect a page number.

Thompson's lecture defined *impulse* as "an action
triggered by the nerves without thought for the
consequences."

Mrs. Peggy Meacham said in her phone interview that
prejudice against young black women is not as
severe as that against young black males.

10d Citing Internet Sources

Identify the Source with Name or Title

Whenever possible, identify the author of an Internet article. Usually, no page number is listed.

Hershel Winthop interprets Hawthorne's stories as the search for holiness in a corrupt Puritan society.

If you can't identify an author, give the article title or Web site information.

One Web site claims that any diet that avoids carbohydrates will avoid some sugars that are essential for the body ("Fad Diets").

Identify the Nature of the Information and Its Credibility

As a service to your reader, indicate your best estimate of the scholarly value of an Internet source. For example, the next citation explains the role of the Center for Communications Policy:

The UCLA Center for Communication Policy, which conducted an intensive study of television violence, has advised against making the television industry the "scapegoat for violence" by advocating a focus on "deadlier and more significant causes: inadequate parenting, drugs, underclass rage, unemployment and availability of weaponry."

Here is another example of an introduction that establishes credibility:

John Armstrong, a spokesperson for Public Electronic Access to Knowledge (PEAK), states:

As we venture into this age of biotechnology, many people predict gene manipulation will be a powerful tool for improving the quality of life. They foresee plants engineered to resist pests, animals designed to produce large quantities of rare medicinals, and humans treated by gene therapy to relieve suffering.

> **NOTE:** To learn more about the source of an Internet article, as in the case immediately above, learn to search out a home page. The address for Armstrong's article is **www. peak.org/~armstroj/america.html#Aims**. By truncating the address to **www.peak.org/** you can learn about the organization that Armstrong represents.

If you are not certain about the credibility of a source, that is, it seemingly has no scholarly or educational basis, do not cite it or describe the source so that readers can make their own judgments:

```
An Iowa nonprofit organization, the Mothers for
Natural Law, says—but offers no proof—that eight
major crops are affected by genetically engineered
organisms: canola, corn, cotton, dairy products,
potatoes, soybeans, tomatoes, and yellow crook-neck
squash ("What's on the Market").
```

Omitting Page and Paragraph Numbers to Internet Citations

In general, you should not list a page number, paragraph number, or screen number to an Internet site.

- You cannot list a screen number because monitors differ.
- You cannot list a page number of a downloaded document because computer printers differ.
- Unless they are numbered in the document, you cannot list paragraph numbers. Besides, you would have to go through and count every paragraph.

The marvelous feature of electronic text is that it's searchable, so your readers can find your quotation quickly with the FIND or SEARCH features. Suppose that you have written the following:

```
The Television Violence Report advises against
making the television industry the "scapegoat for
violence" by advocating a focus on "deadlier and
more significant causes: inadequate parenting,
drugs, underclass rage, unemployment and
availability of weaponry."
```

A reader who wants to investigate further can consult your Works Cited page, find the Internet address (URL), use a browser to locate the article, and use FIND for a phrase, such as *scapegoat for violence*. That's much easier than numbering all the paragraphs, which also means the reader will be required to count through them.

Some academic societies are urging scholars who publish on the Internet to number their paragraphs, and that practice may catch on quickly. Therefore, you should provide a paragraph number if the author of the Internet article has numbered each paragraph.

```
The Insurance Institute for Highway Safety
emphasizes restraint first, saying, "Riding
unrestrained or improperly restrained in a motor
vehicle always has been the greatest hazard for
children" (IIHS, par. 13).
```

Provide a page number only if you find original page numbers burned within the electronic article. For example, a database like JSTOR reproduces original images of works and thereby provides original page numbers, as with the following quotation from an article by Harold R. Walley. Cite these pages just as you would a printed source.

```
One source says the "moralizing and philosophical
speculation" in Hamlet is worthy of examination, but
to Shakespeare these were "distinctly subsidiary to
plot and stage business . . . (Walley 777-778).
```

CHECKLIST USING LINKS TO DOCUMENT INTERNET SOURCES

If you are publishing your project on your own Web page, you have the opportunity to send your readers to various sites by use of hypertext links. If you do so, follow these guidelines:

1. You may activate a hot key (hypertext link) in your document that will automatically send your reader to one of your sources.

2. Identify the linked source clearly so that the reader will know where the link will take them.

3. Be selective and do not sprinkle your document with multiple links to sites all over the Web. You want the reader to stay with you, not wander around on the Internet.

4. The links are part of your documentation, so provide a citation to these linked sources in your Works Cited list.

10e Citing Indirect Sources

Sometimes the writer of a book or article will quote another person from an interview or personal correspondence, and you will want to use that same quotation. For example, in a newspaper article in *USA Today*, page 9A, Karen S. Peterson writes this passage in which she quotes two other people:

> Sexuality, popularity, and athletic competition will create anxiety for junior high kids and high schoolers, Eileen Shiff says. "Bring up the topics. Don't wait for them to do it; they are nervous and they want to appear cool." Monitor the amount of time high schoolers spend working for money, she suggests. "Work is important, but school must be the priority." Parental intervention in a child's school career that worked in junior high may not work in high school, psychiatrist Martin Greenburg adds. "The interventions can be construed by the adolescent as negative, overburdening and interfering with the child's ability to care for himself." He adds, "Be encouraging, not critical. Criticism can be devastating for the teen-ager."

Suppose that you want to use the quotation above by Martin Greenburg. You will need to quote the words of Greenburg and also put Peterson's name in the parenthetical citation as the person who wrote the article, as shown in the following:

```
After students get beyond middle school, they begin
to resent interference by their parents, especially
in school activities. They need some space from Mom
and Dad. Martin Greenburg says, "The interventions
can be construed by the adolescent as negative,
overburdening and interfering with the child's
ability to care for himself" (qtd. in Peterson 9A).
```

On the Works Cited page, Peterson's name will appear on a bibliography entry, but Greenburg's name will not appear there because Greenburg is not the author of the article.

In other words, you need a double reference that introduces the speaker and includes a clear reference to the book or article where you found the quotation or the paraphrased material. Without the reference to Peterson, nobody could find the article. Without the reference to Greenburg, readers would assume that Peterson spoke the words.

> ■ **HINT:** Cite the original source if it is readily available rather than use the double reference.

10f Citing Frequent Page References to the Same Work

If you quote more than once from the same page within a paragraph, and no other citations intervene, you may provide one citation at the end for all the references.

> When the character Beneatha denies the existence of
> God in Hansberry's A Raisin in the Sun, Mama slaps
> her in the face and forces her to repeat after her,
> "In my mother's house there is still God." Then
> Mama adds, "There are some ideas we ain't going to
> have in this house. Not long as I am at the head of
> the family" (37).

Also, when you make frequent references to the same source, you need not repeat the author's name in every instance. Note the following example:

> The consumption of "healing foods," such as those
> that reduce blood pressure, grows in popularity
> each year. Clare Hasler says that when the
> medicinal properties of functional food gains the
> support of clinical evidence, functional foods can
> become an economic weapon in the battle against
> rising health care costs. In addition, functional
> foods may be a promising addition to the diet of
> those suffers from deadly disease. As executive
> director the Functional Foods for Health Program at

the University of Illinois, she claims, "Six of the
ten leading causes of death in the United State are
believed to be related to diet: cancer, coronary
heart disease, stroke, diabetes, atherosclerosis,
and liver disease" ("Western Perspective" 66).

> ■ **NOTE:** If you are citing from two or more novels in your
> paper, let's say Robert Penn Warren's *All the King's Men* and
> *World Enough and Time,* provide both title (abbreviated)
> and page(s) unless the reference is clear: (*Men* 85) and
> (*World* 18–19).

10g Citing Material from Textbooks and Large Anthologies

Reproduced below is a poem that you might find in many literary
textbooks.

The Red Wheelbarrow
so much depends
upon
a red wheel
barrow
glazed with rain
water
beside the white chickens

> *William Carlos Williams*

If you quote lines of the poem, and if that is all you quote from the
anthology, cite the author and page in the text and put a comprehensive entry in the works cited list.

Text:

For Williams, "so much depends" on the red wheel
barrow as it sits "glazed with rain water beside
the white chickens" (780).

Works Cited entry:

Williams, William Carlos. "The Red Wheelbarrow."
    The Compact Bedford Introduction to

Literature. 7th ed. Ed. Michael Meyer. Boston:
Bedford / St. Martin's, 2006. 780.

Suppose, however, that you also take quotations from other poems in the textbook.

Robert Frost calls for escape into the pleasures
of nature, saying "I'm going out to clean the
pasture spring; / I only stop to rake the leaves
away" and invites us to join in, "You come too"
(852-53).

T. S. Eliot describes the fog as a "yellow smoke"
that "Slipped by the terrace, made a sudden leap"
(910).

Now, with three citations to the same anthology, you should list in your Works Cited the anthology used, as edited by Meyer, and also use shortened citations for Williams, Frost, and Eliot with each referring to the lead editor's name, in this case, *Michael Meyer.*

Eliot, T. S. "The Love Song of J. Alfred Prufrock."
    Meyer. 910.
Frost, Robert. "The Pasture." Meyer. 852.
Meyer, Michael, Ed. The Compact Bedford
    Introduction to Literature. 7th ed. Ed.
    Boston: Bedford / St. Martin's, 2006.
Williams, William Carlos. "The Red Wheelbarrow."
    Meyer. 780.

10h Adding Extra Information to In-text Citations

As a courtesy to your reader, add extra information within the citation. Show parts of books, different titles by the same writer, or several works by different writers. For example, your reader may have a different anthology than yours, so a clear reference "(*Great Expectations* 681; chap.4)," will enable the reader to locate the passage. The same is true with a reference to "(*Romeo and Juliet* 2.3.65–68)." The reader will find the passage in almost any edition of Shakespeare's play.

Here's a reference to Herman Melville's *Moby Dick*, showing both page and chapter:

> Melville uncovers the superstitious nature of Ishmael
> by stressing Ishmael's fascination with Yojo, the
> little totem god of Queequeg (71; chap. 16).

One of Several Volumes

These next two citations provide three vital facts: (1) an abbreviation for the title, (2) the volume used, and (3) the page number(s). The Works Cited entry will list the total number of volumes (see pages 202–203).

> In a letter to his Tennessee Volunteers in 1812
> General Jackson chastised the "mutinous and
> disorderly conduct" of some of his troops (Papers
> 2: 348–49).

> Joseph Campbell suggests that man is a slave yet
> also the master of all the gods (Masks 2: 472).

However, if you use only one volume of a multivolume work, you need give only page numbers in the parenthetical reference. Then include the volume number in the Works Cited entry (see pages 202–203):

> Don Quixote's strange adventure with the Knight of
> the Mirrors is one of Cervantes's brilliant short
> tales (1908–14).

If you refer to an entire volume, there is no need for page numbers:

> The Norton Anthology includes masterpieces of the
> ancient world, the Middle Ages, and the Renaissance
> (Mack et al., vol. 1).

Two or More Works by the Same Writer

In this example the writer makes reference to two different novels, both abbreviated. Full titles are *Tess of the D'Urbervilles* and *The Mayor of Casterbridge*.

> Thomas Hardy reminds readers in his prefaces that
> "a novel is an impression, not an argument" and
> that a novel should be read as "a study of man's
> deeds and character" (*Tess* xxii; *Mayor* 1).

If the author appears in the parenthetical citation, place a comma after the author's name "(Hardy, *Tess* xxii; Hardy, *Mayor* 1)." If anything other than a page number appears after the title, follow the title with a comma "(Worth, "Computing," par. 6)."

The complete titles of the two works by Campbell that are referenced in the following example are *The Hero with a Thousand Faces* and *The Masks of God*, a four-volume work.

> Because he stresses the nobility of man, Joseph Campbell suggests that the mythic hero is symbolic of the "divine creative and redemptive image which is hidden within us all . . ." (Hero 39). The hero elevates the human mind to an "ultimate mythogenetic zone—the creator and destroyer, the slave and yet the master, of all the gods" (Masks 1: 472).

Several Authors in One Citation

You may wish to cite several different sources that treat the same topic. Put them in alphabetical order to match that of the works-cited page, or place them in the order of importance to the issue at hand. Separate them with semicolons.

> Several sources have addressed this aspect of gang warfare as a fight for survival, not just for control of the local neighborhood or "turf" (Robertson 98–134; Rollins 34; Templass 561–65).

Additional Information with the Page Number

Your citations can refer to special parts of a page (*footnote, appendix, graph, table*) and can also specify emphasis on particular pages.

> Horton (22, n. 3) suggests that Melville forced the symbolism, but Welston (199–248, esp. 234) reaches an opposite conclusion.

However, use a semicolon to separate the page number from the edition used, a chapter number, or other identifying information "(Wollstonecraft 185; ch. 13, sec. 2)."

10i Punctuating Citations Properly and With Consistency

Keep page citations outside quotation marks but inside the final period, as shown here:

"The benefits of cloning far exceed any harm that
might occur" (Smith 34).

In MLA style, use no comma between the name and the page within the citation (for example, Jones 16–17 *not* Jones, 16–17). Do not use *p.* or *pp.* with the page number(s) in MLA style. However, if an author's name begins a citation to paragraph numbers or screen numbers, *do* include a comma after the author's name (Richards, par. 4) or (Thompson, screens 6–7).

Commas and Periods

Place commas and periods inside quotation marks unless the page citation intervenes. The example below shows: (1) how to put the mark inside the quotation marks, (2) how to interrupt a quotation to insert the speaker, (3) how to use single quotation marks within the regular quotation marks, and (4) how to place the period after a page citation.

"Modern advertising," says Rachel Murphy, "not only
creates a marketplace, it determines values." She
adds, "I resist the advertiser's argument that they
'awaken, not create desires'" (192).

Sometimes you may need to change the closing period to a comma. Suppose you decide to quote this sentence: "Scientific cloning poses no threat to the human species." If you start your sentence with the quotation, you will need to change the period to a comma, as shown:

"Scientific cloning poses no threat to the human
species," declares Joseph Wineberg in a recent
article (357).

However, retain question marks or exclamation marks, and no comma is required:

"Does scientific cloning pose a threat to the human
species?" wonders Mark Durham (546).

Let's look at other examples. Suppose this is the original material:

> The Russians had obviously anticipated neither the quick discovery of the bases nor the quick imposition of the quarantine. Their diplomats across the world were displaying all the symptoms of improvisation, as if they had been told nothing of the placement of the missiles and had received no instructions what to say about them.
>
> *From: Arthur M. Schlesinger, Jr.,* A Thousand Days,
> *(New York: Houghton, 1965) 820.*

Punctuate citations from this source in one of the following methods in accordance with MLA style:

"The Russians," writes Schlesinger, "had obviously anticipated neither the quick discovery of the [missile] bases nor the quick imposition of the quarantine" (820).

Schlesinger notes, "Their diplomats across the world were displaying all the symptoms of improvisation . . ." (820).

Schlesinger observes that the Russian failure to anticipate an American discovery of Cuban missiles caused "their diplomats across the world" to improvise answers as "if they had been told nothing of the placement of the missiles . . ." (820).

Note that the last example correctly changes the capital "T" of "their" to lowercase to match the grammar of the restructured sentence, and it does not use ellipsis points before "if" because the phrase flows smoothly into the text.

Semicolons and Colons

Both semicolons and colons go outside the quotation marks, as illustrated by these three examples:

Zigler admits that "the extended family is now rare in contemporary society"; however, he stresses the greatest loss as the "wisdom and daily support of older, more experienced family members" (42).

```
Zigler laments the demise of the "extended family":
that is, the family suffers by loss of the "wisdom
and daily support of older, more experienced family
members" (42).

Brian Sutton-Smith says, "Adults don't worry
whether their toys are educational" (64);
nevertheless, parents want to keep their children
in a learning mode.
```

The third example, immediately above, shows how to place the page citation after a quotation and before a semicolon.

Use the semicolon to separate two or more works in a single parenthetical reference:

```
(Roman, Dallas 16; Manfred 345)

(Steinbeck, Grapes 24; Stuben xii)
```

Question Marks and Exclamation Marks

When a question mark or an exclamation mark serves a part of the quotation, keep it inside the quotation mark. Put the page citation immediately after the name of the source to avoid conflict with the punctuation mark.

```
Thompson (16) passionately shouted to union
members, "We can bring order into our lives even
though we face hostility from every quarter!"
```

If you place the page number at the and of the quotation, retain the original exclamation mark or question mark, follow with the page reference, and then a sentence period outside the citation.

```
Thompson passionately shouted to union members,
"We can bring order into our lives even though we
face hostility from every quarter!" (16).
```

Retain questions marks and exclamation marks when the quotation begins a sentence, and no comma is required.

```
"We face hostility from every quarter!" declared
the union leader.
```

Question marks may appear inside the closing quotation mark when they are part of the original quotation; otherwise, they go outside.

```
The philosopher Brackenridge (16) asks, "How should
we order our lives?"
```

And

```
The philosopher Brackenridge asks, "How should we
order our lives?" (16).
```

but

```
Did Brackenridge say that we might encounter
"hostility from every quarter" (16)?
```

Single Quotation Marks

When a quotation appears within another quotation, use single quotation marks with the shorter one. The period goes inside both closing quotation marks.

```
George Loffler (32) confirms that "the unconscious
carries the best of human thought and gives man
great dignity, but it also has the dark side so
that we cry, in the words of Shakespeare's Macbeth,
'Hence, horrible shadow! Unreal mockery, hence.'"
```

Remember that the period always goes inside quotation marks unless the page citation intervenes, as shown below:

```
George Loffler confirms that "the unconscious
carries the best of human thought and gives man
great dignity, but it also has the dark side so
that we cry, in the words of Shakespeare's
Macbeth, 'Hence, horrible shadow! Unreal mockery,
hence'" (32).
```

10j Indenting Long Quotations

Set off long prose quotations of four lines or more by indenting one inch or 10 spaces, which is usually two clicks of the tab key. Do not enclose the indented material within quotation marks. If you quote only one

paragraph or the beginning of one, do *not* indent the first line an extra
five spaces. Maintain normal double spacing between your text and the
quoted materials. Place the parenthetical citation *after* the final mark
of punctuation. As shown below, the parenthetical citation might be a
title to an Internet article rather than to page numbers:

> The number of people who need transplants continues
> to increase, but the number of donors fails to meet
> these needs. Tommy G. Thompson, secretary for the
> Department of Health and Human Services commented
> on the current state of organ donation:
>
> > Citing the growing need for organ donation
> > to save and improve lives, Tommy G.
> > Thompson, within his first 100 days as HHS
> > Secretary, announced his commitment to
> > develop a new national effort to encourage
> > organ donation. That commitment, also
> > known as the Gift of Life Donation
> > Initiative, led to 2004's record
> > transplant totals through which the number
> > of transplant candidates who died waiting
> > for an organ fell below 6,000 for the
> > first time in six years. ("New Record")
>
> With the ever increasing number of organ donors
> needed, why don't people give of themselves? The
> most recognized reason for the shortage of donors
> is directly related to the myths that are
> associated with organ and tissue donation.

If you quote more than one paragraph, indent all paragraphs an extra
three (3) spaces or a quarter inch. However, if the first sentence quoted
does not begin a paragraph in the original source do not indent it an extra
three spaces.

> Zigler makes this observation:
>
> > With many others, I am nevertheless
> > optimistic that our nation will eventually
> > display its inherent greatness and
> > successfully correct the many ills that I
> > have touched upon here.

> Of course, much remains that could and should be done, including increased efforts in the area of family planning, the widespread implementation of Education for Parenthood programs, an increase in the availability of homemaker and child care services, and a reexamination of our commitment to doing what is in the best interest of every child in America. (42)

10k Citing Poetry

Quoting Two Lines of Poetry or Less

Incorporate short quotations of poetry (one or two lines) into your text.

> In Part 3 Eliot's "The Waste Land" (1922) remains a springtime search for nourishing water: "Sweet Thames, run softly, for I speak not loud or long" (line 12) says the speaker in "The Fire Sermon," while in Part 5 the speaker of "What the Thunder Said" yearns for "a damp gust / Bringing rain" (73-74).

As the example demonstrates:

1. Set off the material with quotation marks.
2. Indicate separate lines by using a virgule (/) with a space before and after the slash mark.
3. Place line documentation within parentheses immediately following the quotation mark and inside the period. Do not use the abbreviation *l.* or *ll.*, which might be confused with page numbers; use *lines* initially to establish that the numbers represent lines of poetry and thereafter use only the numbers.
4. Use Arabic numerals for books, parts, volumes, and chapters of works; acts, scenes, and lines of plays; cantos, stanzas, and lines of poetry.

■ **NOTE:** For complete information, see "Arabic Numerals," Appendix A, pages 247–248.

Quoting Three Lines of Poetry or More

Set off three or more lines of poetry by indenting one inch or 10 spaces, as shown below. Use double-spaced lines. A parenthetical citation to the lines of indented verse follows the last line of the quotation. If the parenthetical citation will not fit on the last line, place it on the next line, flush with the right margin of the poetry text.

> The king cautions Prince Henry:
>> Thy place in council thou has rudely lost,
>> Which by thy younger brother is supplied,
>> And art almost an alien to the hearts
>> Of all the court and princes of my blood.
>>> (3.2.32–35)

Refer to act, scene, and lines only after you have established Shakespeare's *Henry IV, Part 1* as the central topic of your study; otherwise, write (1H4 3.2.32–35). If you are citing from more than one play, always add an abbreviation for the play (H5 1.1.17–19).

Indenting Turnovers for Long Lines of Poetry

When quoting a line of poetry that is too long for your right margin, indent the continuation line three (3) spaces or a quarter inch more than the greatest indentation.

> Plath opens her poem with these lines:
>> Love set you going like a fat gold watch.
>> The midwife slapped your footsoles, and
>>> your bald cry
>> Took its place among the elements.
>>> (lines 1–3)

You may also indent less to make room for the words:

> Plath opens her poem with these lines:
> Love set you going like a fat gold watch.
> The midwife slapped your footsoles, and your bald cry
> Took its place among the elements. (lines 1–3)

NOTE: For details concerning the use of ellipsis points with poetry, see page 163.

Retaining Internal Quotations within a Block

While you should not use quotation marks around a block quotation, do retain any internal quotation marks:

> With his sonnet "Spring," Shakespeare playfully
> describes the cry of the cuckoo bird:
> > The cuckoo then, on every tree,
> > Mocks married men; for thus sings he,
> >   "Cuckoo!
> > Cuckoo, cuckoo!" O word of fear,
> > Unpleasing to a married ear! (524)

Providing Translations

When a quotation is run into the text, use double quotation marks for translations placed within parentheses but single quotations around a translation without the parentheses:

> Chaucer's setting is spring when "zephyrs ("west
> winds") have breathed softly all about . . ."
> > > (line 5).
> Chaucer's setting is spring when "zephyrs 'west
> winds' have breathed softly all about . . ." (line 5).

Do not place quotation marks for quotations and translations set off from the text in a block.

Place the block of translation below the block of poetry.

> Ramon Magrans translated Lorca poem in a literal
> manner:
> > Alto pinar!
> > Cuatro palomas por el aire van.
> >
> > Cuatro palomas
> > vuelan y tornan
> > Llevan heridas
> > sus cuatro sombras
> >
> > Bajo pinar!
> > Cuatro palomas en la tierra están.

```
Above the pine trees:
Four pigeons go through the air.

Four pigeons
fly and turn round.
They carry wounded
their four shadows.

Below the pine trees:
Four pigeons lie on the earth.
```

10l   Handling Quotations from a Play

Dialogue by two or more characters should be set off from your text, and each set of lines should begin with the character's name, indented one inch or 10 spaces from the left margin and written in all capital letters. Follow the name with a period, space once, and begin the quotation unless the original has different spacing as shown below with the lines of Kreon, which are set to the right. Indent subsequent lines of speech an extra quarter of an inch or three spaces. Start a new line when the dialogue shifts to another character. Note the form of this example:

```
At the end of Oedipus Rex, Kreon chastises Oedipus,
reminding him that he no longer has control over
his own life nor that of his children.
         KREON.    Come now and leave your children.
         OEDIPUS. No! Do not take them from me!
         KREON.    Think no longer
                   That you are in command here, but
                      rather think
                   How, when you were, you served
                      your own destruction.
```

10m   Altering Initial Capitals in Some Quoted Matter

In general, you should reproduce quoted materials exactly, yet one exception is permitted for logical reasons. Restrictive connectors, such as *that* or *because*, create restrictive clauses and eliminate a need for the comma.

Without a comma, the capital letter is unnecessary. In the following example, "The," which is capitalized as the first word in the original sentence, is changed to lowercase because it continues the grammatical flow of the student's sentence.

```
Another writer argues that "the single greatest
impediment to our improving the lives of America's
children is the myth that we are a child-oriented
society" (Zigler 39).
```

Otherwise, write:

```
Another writer argues, "The single greatest . . . ."
```

10n Omitting Quoted Matter with Ellipsis Points

You may omit portions of quoted material with three spaced ellipsis points, as shown in the examples below.

Context

In omitting passages, be fair to the author. Do not change the meaning or take a quotation out of context.

Correctness

Maintain the grammatical correctness of your sentences; that is, avoid fragments and misplaced modifiers. You don't want your readers to misunderstand the structure of the original. When you quote only a phrase, readers will understand that you omitted most of the original sentence, so no ellipsis is necessary.

```
Phil Withim recognizes the weakness in Captain
Vere's "intelligence and insight" into the
significance of his decisions regarding Billy Budd
(118).
```

Omission within a Sentence

Use three ellipsis points (periods) with a space before each and a space after the last.

Phil Withim objects to the idea that "such episodes
are intended to demonstrate that Vere [. . .] has the
intelligence and insight to perceive the deeper
issue" (118).

Omission at the End of a Sentence

If an ellipsis occurs at the end of your sentence, use three periods with
a space before each following a sentence period. That is, you will have
four periods with no space before the first or after the last. A closing quotation mark finishes the punctuation.

R. W. B. Lewis (62) declares that "if Hester has
sinned, she has done so as an affirmation of life,
and her sin is the source of life[. . . ."]

However, if a page citation also appears at the end in conjunction with
the ellipsis, use three periods with a space before each and put the sentence period after the final parenthesis. Thus, you will have three ellipsis points with a space before each, the closing quotation mark followed
by a space, the parenthetical citation, and the period.

R. W. B. Lewis declares that "if Hester has sinned,
she has done so as an affirmation of life, and her
sin is the source of life [. . ." (62).]

Omission at the Beginning of a Sentence

Most style guides discourage the use of ellipsis points for material omitted from the beginning of a source, as shown here:

He states: ["]. . . the new parent has lost the wisdom
and daily support of older, more experienced family
members" (Zigler 34).

The passage would read better without the ellipsis points:

He states that ["]the new parent has lost the wisdom
and daily support of older, more experienced family
members" (Zigler 34).

Omission of Complete Sentences and Paragraphs

Use a closing punctuation mark and three spaced ellipsis points when
omitting one or more sentences from within a long quotation. Here's an

omission in which one sentence ends, another sentence or more is omitted, and a full sentence ends the passage.

```
Zigler reminds us that "child abuse is found more
frequently in a single (female) parent home in
which the mother is working . . . . The
unavailability of quality day care can only make
this situation more stressful" (42).
```

Here is an omission from the middle of one sentence to the middle of another:

```
Zigler reminds us that "child abuse is found more
frequently in a single (female) parent home in
which the mother is working , . . . so the
unavailability of quality day care can only make
this situation more stressful" (42).
```

Omissions in Poetry

If you omit a word or phrase in a quotation of poetry, indicate the omission with three or four ellipsis points just as you would with omissions in a prose passage. However, if you omit a complete line or more from the poem, indicate the omission by a line of spaced periods that equals the average length of the lines. Note that the parenthetical citation shows two sets of lines.

```
Elizabeth Barrett Browning asks:
        Do ye hear the children weeping, O my
            brothers,
        Ere the sorrow comes with years?
    They are leaning their young heads against
        their mothers,
    And that cannot stop their tears.
    . . . . . . . . . . . . . . . . . . . . . . .
    They are weeping in the playtime of the
        others,
    In the country of the free. (1-4, 11-12)
```

Avoid Excessive Use of Ellipsis Points

Many times you can be more effective if you incorporate short phrases rather than quote the whole sprinkled with many ellipsis points. Note how this next passage incorporates quotations without the use of ellipsis.

> The long-distance marriage, according to William
> Nichols, "works best when there are no minor-aged
> children to be considered," the two people are
> "equipped by temperament and personality to spend a
> considerable amount of time alone," and both are
> able to "function in a mature, highly independent
> fashion" (54).

Ellipsis in the Original

If the original passage has ellipsis by the author, and you wish to cut additional words, place brackets around your ellipsis points to distinguish them from the author's ellipsis points. If the original says:

> Shakespeare's innovative techniques in working with revenge tragedy are important in *Hamlet* . . . while the use of a Senecan ghost is a convention of revenge tragedy, a ghost full of meaningful contradictions in calling for revenge is part of Shakespeare's dramatic suspense.

If you cut the middle phrase, use this form:

> One writer says, "Shakespeare's innovative
> techniques in working with revenge tragedy are
> important in *Hamlet*, . . . [. . .] a ghost full of
> meaningful contradictions in calling for revenge is
> part of Shakespeare's dramatic suspense."

10o Altering Quotations with Parentheses and Brackets

You will sometimes need to alter a quotation to emphasize a point or to make something clear. You might add material, italicize an important word, or use the word *sic* (Latin for *thus* or *so*) to alert readers that you have properly reproduced the material even though the logic or the spelling of the original might appear to be in error. Use parentheses or brackets according to these basic rules.

Parentheses

Use parentheses to enclose your comments or explanations that fall outside a quotation, shown in these examples:

The problem with airbags is that children (even those in protective seats) can be killed by the force as the airbag explodes. Boughman (46) urges car makers to "direct the force of automotive airbags underline{upward} against the windshield" (emphasis added).

Roberts (22) comments that "politicians suffer a conflict with honoure" (sic).

Brackets

Use brackets for interpolation, which means to insert your own comment into a text or quotation. The use of brackets signals the insertion. Note the following rules.

Use Brackets to Clarify

This same critic indicates that "we must avoid the temptation to read it [The Scarlet Letter] heretically" (118).

Use Brackets to Establish Correct Grammar within an Abridged Quotation

"John F. Kennedy [was] an immortal figure of courage and dignity in the hearts of most Americans," notes one historian (Jones 82).

He states: "[The] new parent has lost the wisdom and daily support of older, more experienced family members" (Zigler 34).

Use Brackets to Note the Addition of Underlining

He says, for instance, that the "extended family is now rare in contemporary society, and with its demise the new parent has lost the wisdom [my emphasis] and

```
daily support of older, more experienced family
members" (Zigler 42).
```

Use Brackets to Substitute a Proper Name for a Pronoun

```
"As we all know, he [Kennedy] implored us to serve
the country, not take from it" (Jones 432).
```

Use Brackets with Sic to Indicate Errors in the Original

```
Lovell says, "John F. Kennedy, assassinated in
November of 1964 [sic], became overnight an
immortal figure of courage and dignity in the
hearts of most Americans" (62).
```

> ■ **NOTE:** The assassination occurred in 1963. However, do not burden your text with the use of "sic" for historical matter in which misspellings are obvious, as with: "Faire seemely pleasauance each to other makes."

Use Brackets with Ellipsis Points

See the examples on page 164.

10p Formatting the Paper in MLA Style

The format of a research paper consists of the following parts (items 1, 3, and 6 are required):

1. Title page or opening page with title
2. Outline (if required)
3. The text of the paper
4. Content notes
5. Appendix
6. Works Cited

Title Page or Opening Page

A research paper in MLA style does not need a separate title page unless you include an outline, abstract, or other introductory matter. Place your identification in the upper left corner of your opening page, as shown here:

```
Pamela Howell
English 102c, U of A
May 17, 2005

              Creative Marriages

    Judging by recent divorce rates, it would seem
that the traditional marriage fails to meet the
needs. . . .
```

If you write a title page, center the information uniformly, somewhat like this, in the middle of the page:

```
       An Interpretation of Melville's
          Use of Biblical Characters
                In Billy Budd


                      by
               Doris Singleton
      Freshman English II, Section 108b
               Dr. Crampton
              April 23, 2005
```

Outline

Include your outline with the finished manuscript only if your instructor requires it.

The Text of the Paper

Double-space throughout the entire paper. In general, you should *not* use subtitles or numbered divisions for your paper, even if it becomes twenty pages long. Do not start "Notes" or "Works Cited" on this final page of text.

Content Endnotes Page

Label this page with the word "Notes" centered at the top edge of the sheet. Number the notes in sequence with raised superscript numerals to match those within your text. Double-space all entries and double-space between them.

Appendix

Place additional material, if necessary, in an appendix that precedes the Works Cited page. This is the logical location for tables and illustrations, computer data, questionnaire results, complicated statistics, mathematical proofs, or detailed descriptions of special equipment.

Works Cited

Center the heading "Works Cited" one inch from the top edge of the sheet. Continue the page numbering sequence in the upper right corner. Double-space throughout. Use the hanging indention; that is, set the first line of each entry flush left and indent subsequent lines five spaces or one-half inch. Alphabetize by the last name of the author. See page 184 for an example.

10q Writing a Literary Paper in MLA Style

Portions of a sample research paper by Melinda Mosier are reproduced in the pages that follow. This sample demonstrates the form and style of a literary research paper written to the specifications of the MLA style.

Melinda Mosier
Professor Thompson
Humanities 1020
6 April 2005

Listening to Hamlet: The Soliloquies

A soliloquy is a dramatic form of
discourse in which a person reveals inner
thoughts and feelings while alone on stage
or while unaware that others might be within
the range of their voice. But then, the
person might also deliver such a speech
while knowing full well that somebody is
listening. Thus, the dramatic convention has
complications, and when Shakespeare uses it
with a complex character like Hamlet, it
appears in a variety of forms. Critical
authorities have agreed that the soliloquies
reveal the inner feelings of Hamlet (Auden,
Bloom, and Wilson), and they disagree
somewhat in their interpretations. This
study, however, will examine the settings
within which the soliloquies occur and
interpret the direction of Hamlet's remarks—
inward to himself and outward to a perceived
listener.

The first soliloquy occurs in Act 1,
scene 2, lines 133-164, immediately after
King Claudius and Queen Gertrude have left
in a flourish. His mother has just
admonished Hamlet for wearing black after
these many days following the death of his
father, and he has responded with a play on
the word *seems*, indicating in lines 79-89,

Mosier 2

that his mourning clothes are "but the
trappings and the suits of woe," but that he
has within a mournful spirit that is so deep
it "passes show." He is stricken to his core
by sadness.

> Then he is left alone and cries
>> out:
> Oh, that this too too sullied
>> flesh
> would melt, Thaw, and resolve
>> itself into a dew,
> Or that the Everlasting had not
>> fixed
> His canon 'gainst self-slaughter.
>> O God, God,
> How weary, stale, flat and
>> unprofitable
> Seem to me all the uses of this
>> world! (1.2.133-38)

This opening gives its obvious nod toward
suicide and to the inner darkness of his
soul, which even black clothing cannot show
in full force. But Shakespeare uses this
soliloquy for another important purpose—the
son's verbal attack on his mother, Gertrude.
She has just left in a flourish with the
king, her new husband. Hamlet reveals his
disgust with her because she has moved with
"most wicked speed" (1.2.161) to marry
Claudius, her dead husband's brother. Hamlet
sees the union as incest as closes the
soliloquy by saying: "It is not, nor it
cannot come to good: / But break, my heart,

Mosier 3

for I must hold my tongue!" (1.2.163-64).
Some critics, like Ernest Jones, would
suggest that Hamlet is jealous of Claudius
for winning a love that he (Hamlet) wanted,
but that idea is severely weakened by
Hamlet's damning words against her dexterity
within *"incestuous sheets"* (my emphasis).
   The second soliloquy occurs in Act
2.2.576-634). The setting again has great
relevance to Hamlet's words. An actor has
just described how his company would portray
the anguished and agonized cries Hecuba, who
must watch as her husband Priam, the king of
Troy, is hacked to death. Now, Hamlet is
dismayed because a mere actor can show such
passion in a fictional portrayal:

> O, what a rogue and peasant slave
>   am I!
> Is it not monstrous that this
>   player here,
> But in a fiction, in a dream of
>   passion,
> Could force his soul so to his own
>   conceit
> That from her working all his
>   visage wanned,
> Tears in his eyes, distraction in
>   his aspect,
> A broken voice, and his whole
>   function suiting
> With forms to his conceit? And all
>   for nothing!
> For Hecuba!

Mosier 4

> What's Hecuba to him, or he to
>   Hecuba,
> That he should weep for her?
>   (2.2.576–86)

Comparing himself with the actor, Hamlet calls himself a "dull and muddy-mettled rascal" who "can say nothing; no, not for a king, / Upon whose property and most dear life / A damn'd defeat was made. Am I a coward?" (2.2.594-98). Hamlet is tortured in regard to his mother, who is his version of Hecuba (70). Next, Shakespeare uses the soliloquy to set out another comparison—one between a "pigeon-livered" (2.2.604) Prince Hamlet and an active and crafty Prince Hamlet. He recognizes his failure:

> Why, what an ass am I! This is
>   most brave,
> That I, the son of a dear father
>   murdered,
> Prompted to my revenge by heaven
>   and hell,
> Must, like a whore, unpack my
>   heart with words
> And fall a-cursing, like a very
>   drab,
> A scullion!
> Fie upon 't! (2.2.611-16)

But suddenly, Hamlet changes his attitude, saying, "About, my brain!" This means, get busy brain and go to work! So now he plots the play within a play, saying,

Mosier 5

"The play's the thing / Wherein I'll catch
the conscience of the king" (2.2.633-34).

In short, this soliloquy has three
parts, all tied to the setting—praise for a
performer who can act with passion, disgust
with himself for his failure to act, and
then his cunning plan for tricking the king
by using the actors. Yet throughout the
soliloquy he seems to be acting, and
Shakespeare scholar Harold Bloom stresses
that idea, saying:

> So histrionic is all of *Hamlet*
> that we need to develop our
> auditory consciousness to a new
> pitch, if we catch the prince's
> precise accent here. Where all
> is theatricality, our grounds
> for judgment must shift.
> Hamlet's hyperboles mock
> theater itself, in "drown the
> stage with tears." The
> soliloquy becomes a hyperparody
> of soliloquy . . . (30).

The critic W. H. Auden will echo that
sense of "theater" later in this paper, and
Charles Cannon argues that "*Hamlet* is a play
about the play-like deceit of much that
posses for reality" (206).

The third soliloquy, and the most
famous, again has a setting of great import.
This time the king has called for Ophelia to
meet with Hamlet while he and Polonius
eavesdrop nearby. Although Shakespeare has

Mosier 6

given no stage instructions, it seems
reasonable that Hamlet knows the plot, knows
Ophelia is their foil, and knows they are
listening. Thus, this suicidal monologue
could be deception on his part, not a call
for Prozac or death or any mind-altering
alternative. Notice these words:

> To die, to sleep—To sleep—
> perchance to dream: ay, there's
> the rub,
> For in that sleep of death what
> dreams may come
> When we have shuffled off this
> mortal coil,
> Must give us pause. . . .
>
> (3.1.72-76)

He hesitates about rushing into "the
undiscovered country from whose bourn / No
traveler returns" (3.1.87-88), and admits
that "conscience does make cowards of us
all…" (3.1.91). He does not wish to lose his
chance for action, even though some critics,
like Goethe, say a call to action has been
"laid upon a soul unfit for the performance
of it"(154). Thereafter, he performs his own
little drama with Ophelia, knowing that the
king is watching. W. H. Auden has observed
that Hamlet is always "conscious of acting"
(161). His words and actions convince
Ophelia, the king, and Polonius that Hamlet
has lost his sanity:

> Ophelia: O, what a noble mind is
> here o'erthrown!

> The courtier's, soldier's,
>   scholar's, eye, tongue, sword:
> The expectancy and rose of the
>   fair state,
> The glass of fashion and the mould
>   of form,
> Th' observed of all observers,
>   quite, quite down! (3.1.163-64)

Apparently insane, Hamlet can now act decisively in seeking his revenge. Youngson applies the Ganser syndrome to Hamlet, saying the prince has something "notable to gain from being thought mad" so he gives the appearance of psychiatric symptoms (1).

In the fourth soliloquy that begins "'Tis now the very witching time of night" (3.2.419), Hamlet contrasts himself with Nero, a brutal Roman emperor, saying:

> Soft, now to my mother,
>   O heart, lose not they nature, let
>   not ever
> The soul of Nero enter this firm
>   bosom,
> Let me be cruel not unnatural.
> I will speak daggers to her, but
>   use none. (3.2.425-29)

The ghost of his father, after all, has asked him to spare Gertrude but not Claudius. Hamlet is diverted from his task but admits, by the comparison to Nero, that he does not have the stomach for the cruel and unnatural. J. Dover Wilson says his "murderous impulses must be kept in leash.

Mosier 8

True, she deserves the worst he can find it
in his heart to say to her; she may even
deserve death, but it is not for him to
exact it" (244).

We see Hamlet in his fifth soliloquy
still motivating himself, and again
Shakespeare uses a comparison to force the
issue—a prince of Norway versus the prince
of Denmark. The setting is a plain in
Denmark where Fortinbras, the nephew of the
Norwegian king, leads an army across Denmark
to attack a small section of Poland,
fortified by 20,000 soldiers, but in truth
the piece of land is not of great value. The
Norwegian Captain explains, "We go to gain a
little patch of ground / That hath in it no
profit but the name. / To pay five ducats,
five, I would not farm it . . ." (4.4.19-21).
Hamlet recognizes the irony in the contrast—
Fortinbras brazenly fights for what he deems
his even though it has little value but
Hamlet refuses to fight in revenge for the
very real death of his father.

> Witness this army of such mass and
> charge,
> Led by a delicate and tender
> prince,
> Whose spirit, with divine ambition
> puffed,
> Makes mouths at the invisible
> event,
> Exposing what is mortal and unsure

Mosier 9

> To all that fortune, death, and
>   danger dare,
> Even for an eggshell. (4.4.50-56)
> . . . .
>   How stand I then,
> That have a father killed, a
>   mother stained,
> Excitements of my reason and my
>   blood,
> And let all sleep, while to my
>   shame I see
> The imminent death of twenty
>   thousand men
> That for a fantasy and trick of
>   fame
> Go to their graves like beds,
>   fight for a plot
> Whereon the numbers cannot try the
>   cause,
> Which is not tomb enough and
>   continent
> To hide the slain? (4.4.59-68)

Hamlet envisions 20,000 men going to
slaughter and then buried on a plot of land
so small it can't contain all the bodies.
They will fight and die for a worthless
cause while he procrastinates. "O, from this
time forth," he cries, "My thoughts be
bloody, or be nothing worth!" (4.4.69-70).

Thus, Shakespeare has carefully crafted
a setting for each soliloquy, and the device
of *comparison* plays a key role. In the

first, Hamlet cries out that his soul is
darker even than the black funeral garb he
wears because of his mother's incestuous
behavior. In the second, his behavior seems
impotent (and perhaps that's a valid term)
in comparison with the actor who cries so
passionately for Hecuba, a distance historic
figure far removed from Hamlet's recent loss
of a father. In the third, he compares and
contrasts the magnetism of death against
"the dread of something after death, / The
undiscovered country, from whose bourn / No
traveler returns . . ." (3.1.86-87). In the
fourth soliloquy, he reminds himself that he
cannot perform cruel, unnatural acts like
Nero. In the fifth, he stands ashamed of his
inactivity in comparison to an aggressive
Norwegian prince.

In every instance Hamlet compares
himself to someone else—a white knight; a
passionate actor; a vibrant, throbbing human
being; a Nero figure; or an aggressive
soldier. Perhaps W. H. Auden expresses it
best:

> Hamlet lacks faith in God and
> in himself. Consequently he
> must define his existence in
> terms of others, e.g., I am
> the man whose mother married
> his uncle who murdered his
> father. He would like to
> become what the Greek tragic

hero is, a creature of
situation. Hence his inability
to act, for he can only "act,"
i.e., play at possibilities.
He is fundamentally *bored*, and
for that reason he acts
theatrically. (164)

Shakespeare leaves Hamlet alone on stage
in the soliloquies to "act out" his anguish
because he could not act otherwise. Each
setting for each soliloquy was a pivotal but
stifling moment. If we have only the
soliloquies before us, we can see that
Hamlet will fail and "prophesy the election
lights / on Fortinbras" (5.2.392-93), the
man of action, not a man of "acting."

Works Cited

Auden, W. H. *Lectures on Shakespeare.* Ed.
    Arthur Kirsch. Princeton: Princeton
    UP, 2000.

Bloom, Harold. *Hamlet: Poem Unlimited.* New
    York: Riverhead-Penguin, 2003.

Cannon, Charles K. "'As in a Theater'":
    Hamlet in the Light of Calvin's
    Doctrine of Predestination." *Studies
    in English Literature, 1500–1600* 11
    (1971): 203–22. *JSTOR*. 8 Apr. 2005
    <http://www.jstor.org/search>.

Goethe, Johann Wolfgang. "A Soul Unfit."
    Wilhelm Meister's Apprenticeship.
    Trans. Thomas Carlyle. *Hamlet: A
    Norton Critical Edition.* Ed. Cyrus
    Hoy. 2nd ed. New York: Norton, 1992.

Jones, Ernest. "The Oedipus-Complex as an
    Explanation of Hamlet's Mystery: A
    Study in Motive." *The American Journal
    of Psychology* 21.1 (1910): 72–113.
    Shakespeare Navigators. 8 Apr. 2005
    <http://www.clicknotes.com/jones>.

Shakespeare, William. The Tragedy of
    Hamlet, Prince of Denmark. The New
    Folger Library Shakespeare. Ed.
    Barbara A. Mowat and Paul Werstine.
    New York: Washington Square P, 1992.

Wilson, Dover. *What Happens in Hamlet.*
    1935. Cambridge, UK: Cambridge UP, 2001.

Youngson, Robert M. *The Madness of Hamlet
    and Other Extraordinary State of Mind.*
    New York: Carroll & Graf, 1999.

Your Research Project

1. Make a critical journey through your draft with one purpose—to examine your handling of the sources. Have you introduced them clearly so that the reader will know when the borrowing began? Have you closed them with a page citation, as appropriate? Have you placed quotation marks at the beginning and the end of borrowed phrases as well as borrowed sentences.

2. If you have used any Internet sources, look again at the sources to see if the paragraphs on the Internet site are numbered. If so, use the paragraph numbers in your citation(s); if not, use no numbers—not the numbers on any printout and not paragraph numbers if you must count them.

3. Look at your source material to find a table, graph, figure, or photograph that you might insert into your paper as additional evidence. Then consult page 249 to be certain that you have labeled it correctly.

CHAPTER ELEVEN

WORKS CITED: MLA STYLE

After writing your paper, you should begin to finalize your Works Cited page to list your reference materials. List only those materials actually used in your manuscript, including works mentioned within content endnotes and in captions to tables and illustrations. Preparing the Works Cited list will be relatively simple if you have carefully developed your working bibliography as a computer file (see pages 34–35). It will be difficult only if you have not kept publication data on each source cited in the paper.

Keep in mind that on occasion somebody might use your bibliography for research of their own. A documentation system, such as the MLA style, gives all scholars in the field a consistent way to consult the sources. Inaccurate records might prevent an easy retracing of your steps.

Select a heading that indicates the nature of your list.

Works Cited for a list of works including books, articles, films, recordings, Internet sources, and so on that are quoted or paraphrased in the research paper.

Works Consulted if your list includes nonprint items such as an interview, letter, or speech, as well as printed works.

Annotated Bibliography for a list of reverences that includes a description of the contents of each source (see pages 94–98).

Selected Bibliography for a list of readings on the subject.

> ■ **NOTE:** For examples of Works Cited pages, see pages 180 and 184–185. For an example of an annotated bibliography see pages 94–98.

11a Formatting the Works Cited Page

Arrange items in alphabetic order by the surname of the author using the letter-by-letter system. Ignore spaces in the author's surname. Consider the first names only when two or more surnames are identical. Note how the following examples are alphabetized letter by letter.

Bandercloth, Morgan

Dempsey, William R.

Lawrence, Jacob

Lawrence, Melissa

McPherson, James Alan

Saint-Exupéry, Antoine de

St. James, Christopher

When two or more entries cite coauthors that begin with the same name, alphabetize by the last names of the second authors:

Huggins, Marjorie, and Devan Blythe

Huggins, Marjorie, and Stephen Fisher

When no author is listed, alphabetize by the first important word of the title. Imagine lettered spelling for unusual items. For example, "#2 Red Dye" should be alphabetized as though it were "Number 2 Red Dye."

The list of sources may also be divided into separate alphabetized sections for primary and secondary sources, for different media (articles, books, Internet sources), for different subject matter (biography, autobiography, letters), for different periods (Neoclassic period, Romantic period), and for different areas (German viewpoints, French viewpoints, American viewpoints).

Place the first line of each entry flush with the left margin and indent succeeding lines one inch, usually one tab space on the computer or five spaces on a typewriter. Double-space each entry, and also double-space between entries. Use one space after periods and other marks of punctuation.

Set the title, "Works Cited," one inch down from the top of the sheet and double-space between it and the first entry. A sample page is illustrated below.

> **NOTE:** Check your instructor's preference before using italics in place of underlining for titles. If in doubt, use underlining because it prevents ambiguity by its distinctive marking of words and titles.

Masterson 12

Works Cited

Amato, Peter. "Hobbies, Darwinism, and Conceptions
   of Human Nature." *Minerva: An Internet Journal
   of Philosophy*. 6 (2002). 22 Sept. 2005
   <http://www.ul.ie/~philos/vol6/hobbes.html>.

Boyd, Robert, and Joan B. Silk. *How Humans Evolved*.
   3rd ed. New York: Norton, 2003.

Campbell, Joseph. *The Hero with a Thousand Faces*.
   New York: Fine, 1996.

---, *The Masks of God*. 4 vols. New York: Viking,
   1970.

Ehringhaus, Susan, and David Korn. "Conflicts of
   Interest in Human Subjects Research." *Issues
   in Science and Technology Online*. 19.2 (2002).
   20 Sept. 2005 <http://www.nap.edu/issues/19.2/
   ehringhaus.htm>.

Jenkins, Philip. "Catch Me Before I Kill More:
   Seriality as Modern Monstrosity." *Cultural
   Analysis* 3 (2002). 20 Sept. 2005
   <http://socrates.berkeley.edu/%7Ecaforum/
   volume3/vol_article1.html>.

Kourany, Janet A. "A Philosophy of Science for the
   Twenty-First Century." *Philosophy of Science*
   70.1 (2003): 1-14.

Martin, Thomas R. "Religion, Myth, and Community."
    An Overview of Classical Greek History from
    Homer to Alexander. 3 Apr. 1999. 18 Sept. 2003
    <http://www.Perseus.tufts.edu/cgi-bin/
    ptext?doc = Parsees%Adeste%3A1999.04.
    0009%3Ahead%3D%2328>.

Morford, Mark P.O., and Robert J. Lenardon.
    Classical Mythology. 7th ed. New York: Oxford
    UP, 2002.

"North American Mythology." 20 Aug. 2002. 17 Sept.
    2005 <http://www.mythome.org/NorthAm.html>.

11b Bibliography Form — Books

Enter information for books in the following order. Items 1, 3, and 8 are required; add other items according to the circumstances explained in the text that follows.

1. Author(s)
2. Volume number of book
3. Chapter or part of book
4. Name of the series
5. Title of the book
6. Place, publisher, and date
7. Editor, translator, or compiler
8. Page numbers
9. Edition
10. Number of volumes

The following list in alphabetical order explains and gives examples of the correct form for books.

Author's Name

List the author's name, surname first, followed by given name or initials, and then a period:

Truss, Lynn. *Talk to the Hand.* New York: Penguin,
    2006.

Always give authors' names in the fullest possible form, for example, "Grierson, Robert A." rather than "Grierson, R. A." unless, as indicated on the title page of the book, the author prefers initials. If you spell out an abbreviated name, put square brackets around the material added:

Lewis, C[live] S[taples].

With pseudonyms you may add the real name, enclosing the addition in brackets.

```
Carroll, Lewis [Charles Lutwidge Dodgson].
```

Omit a title, affiliation, or degree that appears with the author's name on the title page.

If the title page says:	*In the Works Cited use:*
Sir Edmund Hillary	Hillary, Edmund
Sister Margaret Nelson	Nelson, Margaret
Barton O'Connor, Ph.D.	O'Connor, Barton

However, do provide an essential suffix that is part of a person's name:

```
Justin, Walter, Jr.

Peterson, Robert J, III.
```

Author, Anonymous
Begin with the title. Do not use *anonymous* or *anon*. Alphabetize by the title, ignoring initial articles, *A*, *An*, or *The*.

```
The Song of Roland. Trans. M. S. Merwin. New York:
     Random, 2006.
```

Author, Anonymous But Name Supplied
Alphabetize by the supplied name.

```
[Madison, James.] All Impressments Unlawful and
     Inadmissible. Boston: William Pelham, 1804.
```

Author, Pseudonymous But Name Supplied

```
Slender, Robert [Freneau, Philip]. Letters on
     Various and Important Subjects. Philadelphia:
     D. Hogan, 1799.
```

Author, Listed by Initials with Name Supplied

```
Rowling, J[oanne] K[athleen]. Harry Potter and the
     Half-Blood Prince. New York: Scholastic, 2005.
```

Authors, two

> Middleton, Kent R., and William E. Lee Schwartz.
> > *The Law of Public Communication.* Boston: Allyn
> > & Bacon, 2006.

Authors, Three

> Slywotzky, Adrian, Richard Wise, and Karl Weber.
> > *How to Grow When Markets Don't.* New York:
> > Warner, 2003.

Authors, More Than Three

Use *et al.*, which means "and others," or list all the authors. See the two examples that follow:

> Garrod, Andrew C., et al. *Adolescent Portraits:*
> > *Identity, Relationships, and Challenges.* 5th
> > ed. Boston: Allyn & Bacon, 2005.
> Marzanno, Robert J., Jennifer S. Norford, Diane E.
> > Paynter, Debra J. Pickering, and Barbara B.
> > Gaddy. *Handbook for Classroom Instruction That*
> > *Works.* New York: Prentice Hall, 2004.

Author, Corporation, or Institution

A corporate author can be an association, a committee, or any group or institution when the title page does not identify the names of the members.

> American Medical Association. *Health Professions*
> > *Career and Education Directory 2005-2006.* New
> > York: Random, 2005.

List a committee or council as the author even when the organization is also the publisher, as in this example:

> Consumer Reports. *Consumer Reports Electronics*
> > *Buying Guide 2006.* New York: Consumer Reports,
> > 2006.

Author, Two or More Books by the Same Author

When an author has two or more works, do not repeat his or her name with each entry. Rather, insert a continuous three-dash line flush with the left margin, followed by a period. Also, list the works alphabetically by the title (ignoring *a*, *an*, and *the*), not by the year of publication. In the following example, the *B* of *Bird's-Eye* precedes the *K* of *Key*.

> Freedman, J. F. *Above the Law*. New York: Signet,
>   2001.
> ⸺. *Bird's-Eye View*. New York: Warner, 2001.
> ⸺. *Fallen Idols*. New York: Warner, 2004.

The three dashes stand for exactly the same name(s) as in the preceding entry. However, do not substitute three hyphens for an author who has two or more works in the bibliography when one is written in collaboration with someone else:

> Sagan, Carl. *Contact*. New York: Pocket, 1997.
> ⸺. *Cosmos*. New York: Ballantine, 1985.
> Sagan, Carl, and Ann Druyan. *Shadows of Forgotten
>   Ancestors: A Search for Who We Are*. New York:
>   Random, 1993.

If the person edited, compiled, or translated the work that follows on the list, place a comma after the three hyphens and write *ed.*, *comp.*, or *trans.* before you give the title. This label does not affect the alphabetic order by title.

> Finneran, Richard J., ed. *Editing Yeats's Poems*.
>   New York: St. Martin's, 1983.
> ⸺, ed. *Yeats Reader*. New York: Scribner, 2002.

Author, Two or More Books by the Same Authors

When you cite two or more books by the same authors, provide the names in the first entry only. Thereafter, use three hyphens, followed by a period.

> Axelrod, Rise B., and Charles R. Cooper. *Concise
>   Guide to Writing*. 3rd ed. Boston: St.
>   Martin's, 2002.
> ⸺. *Reading Critically, Writing Well*. 6th ed.
>   Boston: St. Martin's, 2002.

Alphabetized Works, Encyclopedias, and Biographical Dictionaries

Treat works arranged alphabetically as you would an anthology or collection, but omit the name of the editor(s), the volume number, place of publication, publisher, and page number(s). If the author is listed, begin the entry with the author's name; otherwise, begin with the title of the article. If the article is signed with initials, look elsewhere in the work for a complete name. Well-known works, such as the first two examples that follow, need only the edition and the year of publication.

"Kiosk." *The American Heritage College Dictionary.*
    4th ed. 2004.
Moran, Joseph. "Weather." The World Book
    Encyclopedia. 2005 ed.

If you cite a specific definition from among several, add *Def.* (Definition), followed by the appropriate number/letter of the definition.

"Level." Def. 4a. *The American Heritage College*
    Dictionary. 4th ed. 2004.

Less-familiar reference works need a full citation, as shown in this next example:

"Infections." *The American Medical Association*
    Family Medical Guide. 4th ed. Ed. Charles B.
    Clayman. New York: Random, 2004.
"Clindamycin." *Complete Guide to Prescription and*
    Nonprescription Drugs 2005. Eds. H. Winter
    Griffith and Stephen Moore. New York: Penguin,
    2004.

Place within quotation marks the titles to a synopsis or description of a novel or drama, even though the novel or the drama would normally be underscored or italicized.

"Oedipus the King." *The Compact Bedford*
    Introduction to Literature. Ed. Michael Meyer.
    Boston: St. Martin's, 2006. 1049-91.

Anthology, Component Part

In general, works in an anthology have been published previously and collected by an editor. Supply the names of authors as well as editors. Almost always cite the author first. Many times the prior publication data on a specific work may not be readily available; therefore, use this form:

> Reagon, Bernice. "Black Music in Our Hands." *The*
> *Conscious Reader*. Eds. Caroline Shrodes, Harry
> Finestone, and Michael Shugrue. 9th ed. New
> York: Longman, 2003. 345-49.

Provide the inclusive page numbers for the piece, not just the page or pages that you have cited in the text.

> **NOTE:** If you use several works from the same anthology, you can shorten the citation by citing the short work and by making cross references to the larger one, see "Cross-References," page 193.

Use the following form if you can quickly identify original publication information. Conform to the rules given in the following examples. Note that the page numbers in the *New Yorker* were unavailable in the reprint:

> "Soup." *New Yorker* Jan. 1989: n. pag. Rpt. in Rise
> B. Axelrod and Charles R. Cooper. *The St.*
> *Martin's Guide to Writing*. Short 6th ed.
> Boston: Bedford, 2001. 132-34.
> Elder, Lonne. "Ceremonies in Dark Old Men." *New*
> *Black Playwrights: An Anthology*. Ed. William
> Couch, Jr. Baton Rouge: Louisiana State UP,
> 1968. 55-72.

If you cite lines from Aristophanes' drama *Lysistrata* in your paper, write this entry:

> Aristophanes. *Lysistrata*. Trans. Douglass Parker.
> New York: Signet, 2006. 30-39.

If you cite material from a chapter of one volume in a multi-volume set, write an entry like these:

> Child, Harold. "Jane Austen." *The Cambridge History
> of English Literature*. Ed. A. W. Ward and A.
> R. Waller. Vol. 12. London: Cambridge UP,
> 1927.

Although not required, you may also provide the total number of volumes:

> Saintsbury, George. "Dickens." *The Cambridge
> History of English Literature*. Ed. A. W. Ward
> and A. R. Waller. Vol. 13. New York: Putnam's,
> 1917. 14 vols.

The Bible

Do not underscore or italicize the word Bible or the books of the Bible. Common editions need no publication information, but do underscore or italicize special editions of the Bible.

> The Bible. [Denotes King James version]
> The Bible. The Old Testament. CD-ROM. Audio Bible,
> 2003.
> The Bible. Revised Standard Version.
> *The Geneva Bible*. 1560. Facsim. rpt. Madison: U of
> Wisconsin P, 1961.
> *NIV [New International Version] Study Bible*.
> Personal Size Revised Edition. Np.: Zondervan,
> 2002.

A Book Published before 1900

For older books that are now out of print, you may omit the publisher. Use a comma, not a colon, to separate the place of publication from the year. If it has no date listed, use *nd*. If it has no place mentioned, use *np*.

> Dewey, John. *The School and Society*. Chicago, 1899.

Chapter or Part of the Book

List the chapter or part of the book on the Works Cited page only when it is separately edited, translated, or written, or when it demands special attention. For example, if you quote from a specific chapter of a book, let's say Chapter 6 of Frank McCourt's book, the entry should read:

McCourt, Frank. *Teacher Man: A Memoir*. New York:
     Scribner, 2005.

Your in-text citation will have listed specific page numbers, so there is no reason to mention a specific chapter, even though it is the only portion of McCourt's book that you read.

> **NOTE:** If you cite from an anthology or collection, list the title of the specific story, poem, essay, etc. See "Anthology, Component Part," pages 190–191, or "Collection, Component Part," page 192.

Classical Works

Homer. *The Odyssey*. Trans. T. E. Lawrence. New
     York: Barnes, 2004.

You are more likely to find a classic work in an anthology, which would require this citation:

Spenser, Edmund. *The Faerie Queen*. *The Norton
     Anthology of Poetry*. Ed. Margaret Ferguson,
     Mary Jo Salter, and John Stallworthy. New
     York: Norton, 2005. 165–89.

Collection, Component Part

If you cite from one work in a collection of works by the same author, provide the specific name of the work and the corresponding page numbers. This next entry cites one story from a collection of stories by the same author:

Anderson, Mark. "The Sharp Razor of a Willing
     Conceit [1593-1598]." *Shakespeare by Another
     Name*. New York: Gotham, 2005. 272–309.

Cross-References to Works in a Collection

If you are citing several selections from one anthology or collection, provide a full reference to the anthology (as explained on pages 190–191) and then provide references to the individual selections by providing the author and title of the work, the last name of the editor of the collection, and the inclusive page numbers used from the anthology.

```
Elbow, Peter, and Pat Belanoff. Being a Writer.
    Boston: McGraw, 2003.
Koo, Eunsook. "Exploring the Writing Process."
    Elbow and Belanoff 181.
Spencer, Beth. "The Act of Writing as Prayer."
    Elbow and Belanoff 126-28.
Wilbur, Richard. "The Writer." Elbow and Belanoff 220.
```

Note also the following examples in which the first entry refers to the one that follows:

```
Eliot, George. "Art and Belles Lettres."
    Westminster Review. USA ed. April 1856. Partly
    rpt. Eliot, A Writer's Notebook.
---. A Writer's Notebook, 1854-1879, and
    Uncollected Writings. Ed. Joseph Wiesenfarth.
    Charlottesville: UP of Virginia, 1981.
```

Add an abbreviated title to the cross-reference if you list two or more works under the editor's name.

```
Angelou, Maya. "Uncle Willie." Axelrod and Cooper,
    Guide 82-86.
Axelrod, Rise B., and Charles R. Cooper. Reading
    Critically, Writing Well. 5th ed. New York:
    St. Martin's, 1999.
---. The St. Martin's Guide to Writing. Short 6th
    ed. Boston: Bedford, 1997.
Forster, E. M. "My Wood." Axelrod and Cooper,
    Reading 111-14.
Wolff, Tobias. "On Being a Real Westerner." Axelrod
    and Cooper, Guide 33-35.
```

Edition

Indicate the edition used, whenever it is not the first, in Arabic numerals (*3rd ed.*), by name (*Rev. ed.*, *Abr. ed.*), or by year (*1999 ed.*), without further punctuation:

> Agur, Anne M. *Grant's Atlas of Anatomy*. 11th ed. Philadelphia: Lippincott, 2004.

Indicate that a work has been prepared by an editor, not the original author:

> Melville, Herman. *Moby-Dick*. Ed. with Intro. by Alfred Kazin. 2nd Ed. Boston: Houghton, 1956.

If you wish to show the original date of the publication, place the year immediately after the title, followed by a period. Note: the title of an edition in a series is capitalized.

> Hardy Thomas. *Far from the Madding Crowd*. 1874. Ed. Rosemarie Morgan and Shannon Russell. A Penguin Classic Ed. New York: Penguin, 2006.

Editor, Translator, Illustrator, or Compiler

If the name of the editor or compiler appears on the title page of an anthology or compilation, place it first:

> Mitchell, Douglas R., and Judy L. Brunson-Hadley, eds. *Ancient Burial Practices in the American Southwest*. Albuquerque: U of New Mexico P, 2004.

If your in-text citation refers to the work of the editor, illustrator, or translator (e.g., "The Ciardi edition caused debate among Dante scholars") use this form with the original author listed after the work, preceded by the word *By*:

> Birk, Sandow, and Marcus Sanders, trans. *The Purgatorio*. By Dante. San Francisco: Chronicle, 2005.
> Kalman, Maira, illus. *The Elements of Style*. By William Strunk, Jr. and E. B. White. New York: Penguin, 2005.

Jowett, John, William Montgomery, Gary Taylor, and
    Stanley Wells, eds. *The Oxford Shakespeare:*
    The Complete Works. 2nd ed. Oxford: Clarendon,
    2005.

Otherwise, mention an editor, translator, or compiler of a collection *after* the title with the abbreviations *Ed.*, *Trans.*, or *Comp.*, as shown here:

Yeats, W. B. *The Poetry of W. B. Yeats*. Ed. Michael
    Faherty. New York: Palgrave Macmillan, 2005.

Encyclopedia and Reference Books

Ward, Norman. "Saskatchewan." *Encyclopedia*
    Americana. 2006 ed.

> ■ **NOTE:** See also "Alphabetical Works, Encyclopedias, and Biographical Dictionaries" on page 189 and "Citing Sources Found on CD-ROM," pages 225–228.

Introduction, Preface, Foreword, or Afterword

If you are citing the person who has written the introduction to a work by another author, start with the name of the person who wrote the preface or forewarn. Give the name of the part being cited, neither underscored nor enclosed within quotation marks. Place the name of the author in normal order after the title preceded by the word *By*. Follow with publication information and end with the inclusive page numbers:

Shakur, Afeni. Foreword. *Thru My Eyes*. By Gobi. New
    York: Atria, 2005. viii–ix.
Maisel, Eric. Introduction. *A Writer's Paris*. By
    Maisel. Cincinnati: Writer's Digest, 2005.
    1–4.

If the author has written the prefatory matter, not another person, use only the author's last name after the word *By*.

LaHaye, Tim, and Jerry B. Jenkins. Prologue. *The*
    Regime: Evil Advances before They Were Left
    Behind. By Lahaye and Jenkins. Wheaton, IL:
    Tyndale, 2005. ix–xiv.

Use the form above only if you cite from the prologue and not the main text.

Manuscript or Typescript

```
Chaucer, Geoffrey. The Canterbury Tales. Harley ms.
     7334. British Museum, London.
Tabares, Miguel. "Voices from the Ruins of the
     Aztecs." Unpublished essay, 2006.
```

NOTE: For more details about this type of citation, see "Chapter or Part of the Book," page 192, and "Anthologies," page 190.

Page Number(s) to a Section of a Book
Cite pages to help a reader find a particular section of a book.

```
Coyne, Kevin. "The Home Front, 1942-1944." Marching
     Home. New York: Viking, 2003. 75-88.
```

Play, Classical

```
Shakespeare, William. Titus Andronicus. Ed. Thomas
     L. Berger. Rpt. of the 1594 ed. Shakespeare
     Quartos. New York: Oxford UP, 2006.
```

Today, classical plays are usually found in anthologies, which will require this form:

```
Shakespeare, William. Othello, The Moor of Venice.
     The Compact Bedford Introduction to Literature.
     Ed. Michael Meyer. New York: Bedford / St.
     Martin's, 2006. 1112-1192.
```

Play, Modern
Contemporary plays may be published independently or as part of a collection.

```
Mamet, David. Romance. New York: Knopf, 2005.
```

Poem, Classical

Classical poems are usually translated, so you will often need to list a translator and/or editor. If the work is one part of a collection, show which anthology you used.

Dante. *The Divine Comedy.* Trans. John Ciardi. New
York: NAL, 2003.

Dante. *Inferno. The Divine Comedy.* Trans. John
Ciardi. *The Norton Anthology of World
Masterpieces.* Ed. Sarah Lawall et al. New
York: Norton, 1999. 1303-1429.

NOTE: If you cite the translator's or editor's preface or notes
to the text, put the name of the translator or editor first.
See page 194.

Poem, Modern Collection

Use this form that includes the inclusive page numbers if you cite one short poem from a collection:

Stepanek, Mattie J. T., "Splash-Adventure."
Reflections of a Peacemaker. Kansas City:
Andrews McMeel, 2005. 120-21.

Use this next form if you cite from one book-length poem:

Eliot, T. S. *Four Quartets. The Complete Poems and
Plays 1909-1950.* New York: Harcourt, 1952.
115-45.

Do not cite specific poems and pages if you cite several different poems of the collection. Your in-text citations should cite the specific poems and page numbers (see pages 157–160). Your Works Cited entry would then list only the name of the collection.

Eliot, T. S. *The Complete Poems and Plays
1909-1950.* New York: Harcourt, 1952.

Publication Information: Place, Publisher, and Date

Indicate the place of publication, the publisher, and the year of publication:

```
Safire, William. How Not to Write: The Essential
    Misrules of Grammar. New York: Norton, 2005.
```

Include the abbreviation for the state or country only if necessary for clarity:

```
Merwin, W. S. Migration: New and Selected Poems.
    Port Townsend, WA: Copper, 2005.
```

If more than one place of publication appears on the title page, the first city mentioned is sufficient. If successive copyright dates are given, use the most recent (unless your study is specifically concerned with an earlier, perhaps definitive, edition). A new printing does not constitute a new edition. For example, if the text has a 1940 copyright date and a 1975 printing, use 1940 unless other information is given, such as: "facsimile printing" or "1975 third printing rev."

```
Bell, Charles Bailey, and Harriett P. Miller. The
    Bell Witch: A Mysterious Spirit. 1934. Facsim.
    ed. Nashville: Elder, 1972.
```

If the place, publisher, date of publication, or pages are not provided, use one of these abbreviations:

n.p.   No place of publication listed

n.p.   No publisher listed

n.d.   No date of publication listed

n. pag.   No pagination listed

```
Lewes, George Henry. The Life and Works of Goethe.
    1855. 2 vols. Rpt. as vols. 13 and 14 of The
    Works J. W. von Goethe. Ed. Nathan Haskell
    Dole. London: Nicolls, n.d. 14 vols.
Nelson, Marilyn. "Forget Him Not. Though if I
    Could, I Would." A Wreath for Emmett Till.
    Boston: Houghton Mifflin, 2005. N. pag.
```

Provide the publisher's name in a shortened form, such as "Bobbs" rather than "Bobbs-Merrill Co., Inc." A publisher's special imprint name should be joined with the official name, for example, Anchor-Doubleday.

```
Berry, Mary Frances. "Voices of Ex-Slaves." My Face
    Is Black Is True. New York: Knopf, 2005.
    93-121.
```

> **NOTE:** Abbreviations to publisher's names can be shortened to the key word. For example, Delray Education Publishers would simply be listed as "Delray."

Republished Book

If you are citing from a republished book, such as a paperback version of a book published originally in hardback, provide the original publication date after the title and then provide the publication information for the book from which you are citing.

```
Vonnegut, Kurt. Breakfast of Champions. 1973. New
    York: Delta, 1999.
```

Although it is not required, you may wish to provide supplementary information. Give the type of reproduction to explain that the republished work is, for example, a facsimile reprinting of the text:

```
Hooker, Richard. Of the Lawes of Ecclesiasticall
    Politie. 1594. Facsim. rpt. Amsterdam: Teatrum
    Orbis Terrarum, 1971.
```

Give facts about the original publication if the information will serve the reader. In this next example the republished book was originally published under a different title:

```
Arnold, Matthew. "The Study of Poetry." Essays:
    English and American. Ed. Charles W. Eliot.
    1886. New York: Collier, 1910. Rpt. of the
    General Introduction to The English Poets. Ed.
    T. H. Ward. 1880.
```

Screenplay

> Linklater, Richard, Kim Krizan and Julie Delpy.
> *Before Sunrise and Before Sunset.* Screenplay.
> New York: Knopf, 2005.

Series, Numbered and Unnumbered

If the work is one in a published series, show the name of the series, abbreviated, without quotation marks or italics, the number of this work in Arabic numerals and a period:

> Wallerstein, Ruth C. *Richard Crashaw: A Study in*
> *Style and Poetic Development.* U of Wisconsin
> Studies in Lang. and Lit. 37. Madison: U of
> Wisconsin P, 1935.

Sourcebooks and Casebooks

> McGovern, Robert J. "Superior People Skills." *Bring*
> *Your 'A' Game.* Naperville, IL: Sourecbooks,
> 2005. 119–33.

If you can identify the original facts of publication, include that information also:

> Ellmann, Richard. "Reality." *Yeats: The Man and the*
> *Masks.* New York: Macmillan, 1948. Rpt. in
> Yeats: A Collection of Critical Essays. Ed.
> John Unterecker. Twentieth Century Views.
> Englewood Cliffs: Prentice, 1963. 163–74.

> ■ **NOTE:** If you cite more than one article from a casebook, use cross references, see page 193.

Title of the Book

Show the title of the work, underscored or italicized, followed by a period. Separate any subtitle from the primary title by a colon and one space even though the title page has no mark of punctuation or the card catalog entry has a semicolon:

```
Carter, Jimmy. Our Endangered Values: America's
     Moral Crisis. New York: Simon & Schuster,
     2005.
```

If an italicized title to a book incorporates another title that normally receives italics, do not underscore or italicize the shorter title nor place it within quotation marks. In the title below, <u>Absalom and Acidophil</u> is the shorter title; it does not receive italics.

```
Schilling, Bernard N. Dryden and the Conservative
     Myth: A Reading of Absalom and Acidophil. New
     Haven: Yale UP, 1961.
```

■ **NOTE:** See "Titles within Titles," page 252 for additional instructions.

Title of a Book in Another Language
In general, use lowercase letters for foreign titles except for the first major word and proper names. Provide a translation in brackets if you think it necessary (e.g., <u>Étranger</u> [*The Stranger*] or Praha [Prague]).

```
Eco, Umberto. La misteriosa llama de la reina
     loana. Orlando, FL: Harcourt, 2005.
Castex, P. G. Le rouge et le noir de Stendhal.
     Paris: Sedes, 1967.
```

■ **NOTE:** *Le rouge et le noir* is the shorter title within a long title, thus it does not receive italics; compare with the title immediately below that requires italics because there is no additional title within the title.

```
Levowitz-treu, Micheline. L'amour et la mort chez
     Stendhal. Aran: Editions due Grand Chéne,
     1978.
```

Translator
List the translator's name first only if the translator's work (preface, foreword, afterword, notes) is the focus of your study.

```
Marquez, Gabriel Garcia. Memories of My Melancholy
    Whores. Trans. Edith Grossman. New York:
    Knopf, 2005.
Jowett, Benjamin, trans. The Republic. By Plato.
    New York: Barnes & Noble, 2004.
```

Volumes

If you are citing from only one volume of a multi volume work, provide the number of that volume in the works cited entry with information for that volume only. In your text, you will need to specify only page numbers, for example, "(Borgese 45–46)."

```
Chircop, Aldo, and Moira L. McConnell, eds. Ocean
    Yearbook. Vol. 19. Chicago: U of Chicago P,
    2005.
```

Although additional information is not required, you may provide the inclusive page numbers, the total number of volumes, and the inclusive dates of publication.

```
Daiches, David. "The Restoration." A Critical
    History of English Literature. 2nd ed. Vol. 2.
    New York: Ronald, 1970. 537–89. 2 vols.
```

If you are citing from two or more volumes of a multi volume work, your in-text citation will need to specify volume and page (2: 320–321); then the Works Cited entry will need to show the total number of volumes in Arabic numerals, as shown here:

```
Hersen, Michel. Comprehensive Handbook of
    Psychological Assessment. 4 vols.
    Indianapolis: Wiley, 2003.
```

If you are citing from volumes that were published over a period of years, provide the inclusive dates at the end of the citation. Should the volumes still be in production, write *to date* after the number of volumes and leave a space after the hyphen which follows the initial date.

```
Parrington, Vernon L. Main Currents in American
    Thought. 3 vols. New York: Harcourt, 1927–32.
```

```
Cassidy, Frederic, ed. Dictionary of American
    Regional English. 3 vols. to date. Cambridge:
    Belknap-Harvard UP, 1985-date.
```

If you are using only one volume of a multi volume work and the volume has an individual title, you can cite the one work without mentioning the other volumes in the set.

```
Crane, Stephen. Wounds in the Rain. Stephen Crane:
    Tales of War. Charlottesville: UP of Virginia,
    1970. 95-284.
```

As a courtesy to the reader, you may include supplementary information about an entire edition.

```
Crane, Stephen. Wounds in the Rain. Stephen Crane:
    Tales of War. Charlottesville: UP of Virginia,
    1970. Vol. 6 of The University of Virginia
    Edition of the Works of Stephen Crane. Ed.
    Fredson Bowers. 95-284. 10 vols. 1969-76.
```

11c Bibliography Form — Periodicals

For journal or magazine articles, use the following order:

1. Author(s)
2. Title of the article
3. Name of the periodical
4. Series number (if it is relevant)
5. Volume number (for journals)
6. Issue number (if needed)
7. Date of publication
8. Page numbers

These items are explained and shown in the following alphabetized list.

Abstract in an Abstracts Journal

If you have cited from an abstract found in a journal devoted to abstracts, not full articles, begin the citation with information on the original work and then give information on the abstracts journal. Use either item number or page number according to how the journal provides the abstracts.

    Haynie, Donald T., et al. "Polypeptide Multilayer
        Films." *Biomacromolecules* 6 (2005): 2895-2913.
        Chemical Abstracts 98 (2005): item 5523.

Add the word *Abstract* if the title does not make clear that you have used an abstract, not a full article.

    Gryeh, John H., et al. "Patterns of Adjustment
        among Children of Battered Women." *Journal of
        Consulting and Clinical Psychology* 68 (2000):
        84-94. Abstract. PsycLIT 2000-13544.

Use the next form when you cite from *Dissertation Abstracts International* (*DAI*). The page number features A, B, or C to designate the series used: A Humanities, B Sciences, C European dissertations. Before volume 30 (1969) the title was *Dissertation Abstracts*, so use *DA* for those early volumes.

    Nicholson, Andre Wesley. "Criticisms and Critiques:
        An Analysis of Proofreading Marks of College
        English Professors." Diss. Southern Tech. U,
        2005. DAI 66(2005): 2957D.

> ■ **NOTE:** See page 231 for citation information from the full text of a dissertation. See also "Electronic Abstracts," page 227.

Author(s)

Show the author's name flush with the left margin, without a numeral and with succeeding lines indented five spaces. Enter the surname first, followed by a comma, followed by a given name or initials, followed by a period:

    Burden, Barry C., and Casey A. Klofstad. "Affection
        and Cognition in Party Identification."
        Political Psychology 26.6 (Dec. 2005): 869-86.

Author, Anonymous

"Time Capsule: 1938." *Reminisce*. July/Aug. 2005:
   14-16.

Interview, Published

Skaggs, Ricky. Interview with John McManus. "Ricky
   Skaggs: Bluegrass Man Conquers Cool." *Oxford
   American* Summer 2005: 26-31.

Journal, with All Issues for a Year Paged Continuously

Boardman, Jason D., et al. "Race Differentials in
   Obesity: The Impact of Place." *Journal of
   Health & Social Behavior* 46.3 (2005): 229-43.

Journal, with Each Issue Paged Anew

Add the issue number after the volume number because page numbers
alone are not sufficient to locate the article within a volume of six or 12
issues when each issue has separate pagination. Adding the month or sea-
son with the year will also serve the researcher.

Stiglitz, Joseph E. "The Ethical Economist."
   Foreign Affairs 84.6 (Nov./Dec. 2005): 128-34.

If a journal uses only an issue number, treat it as a volume number:

Lee, Cheng Min. "China's Rise, Asia's Dilemma." *The
   National Interest* 81 (Fall 2005): 88-94.

Loose-leaf Collection

If the article is reprinted in an information service that gathers together
several articles on a common topic, use the form shown in the following example.

Cox, Rachel S. "Protecting the National Parks." *The
   Environment*. *CQ Researcher* 16 July 2000:
   523 + . Washington, DC: Congressional
   Quarterly, 2000. No. 23.

Magazine

With magazines, the volume number offers little help for finding an article. For example, one volume of *Time* (52 issues) will have page 16 repeated 52 times. For this reason, you need to insert an exact date (month and day) for weekly and fortnightly (every two weeks) publications. Do not list the volume and issue numbers.

> Lim, Paul J. "The Dollar's Draw." *U.S. News & World*
> *Report* 28 Nov. 2005: 36.

The month suffices for monthly and bimonthly publications:

> Connell, Evan S. "Lost in Uttar Pradesh." *Harper's*
> Dec. 2005: 76-84.

Supply inclusive page numbers (202–09, 85–115, or 1112–24), but if an article is paged here and there throughout the issue (for example, pages 74, 78, and 81–88), write only the first page number and a plus sign with no intervening space:

> Awad, Mona. "If Not Winter, Then Wine." *Utne*
> Nov./Dec. 2005: 92 + .

Microform

Some reference sources, such as *NewsBank*, republishes articles on microfiche. If you use such a microform, enter the original publication information first and then add the pertinent information about the microform, as shown next.

> Chapman, Dan. "Panel Could Help Protect Children."
> <u>Winston-Salem Journal</u> 14 Jan 1990: 14.
> *Newsbank: Welfare and Social Problems* 12
> (1990): fiche 1, grids A8-11.

Name of the Periodical

Give the name of the journal or magazine in full, underscored or italicized, and with no following punctuation. Omit any introductory article, such as *The*.

> Marx, Gary T. "Soft Surveillance." *Dissent* Fall
> 2005: 36-43.

Notes, Editorials, Queries, Reports, Comments, Letters

Magazine and journals publish many pieces that are not full-fledged articles. Identify this type of material if the title of the article or the name of the journal does not make clear the nature of the material (e.g., "Letter" or "Comment").

> Bly, Adam. "Science in 2006." Comment. *SEED* 2.2
> (Dec./Jan. 2006): 10.
> Perina, Kaja. "From the Book of Jobs." Editor's
> note. *Psychology Today* 38.6 (Dec. 2005): 5.
> Maltby, Richard E., Jr. "Letter Drop." Puzzle.
> *Harper's* Dec. 2005: 99.

Reprint of a Journal Article

> Vail, Kathleen. "Climate Control." *American School*
> *Board Journal* 192.6 (June 2005): 12–19. Rpt.
> in *Education Digest* Dec. 2005: 4–11.

Review, in a Magazine, Newspaper, or Journal

Name the reviewer and the title of the review. Then write *Rev. of* and the title of the work being reviewed, followed by a comma, and the name of the author or producer. If necessary, identify the nature of the work within brackets immediately after the title.

> Bowen, Peter. "Casualties of Fame." Rev. of *Capote*,
> by Bennett Miller. *Filmmaker*. 14.1 (Fall
> 2005): 56–59.

If the name of reviewer is not provided, begin the entry with the title of the review.

> "Pentax Optio WP." Rev. of Pentax Optio WP. *Digital*
> *Living* Dec. 2005: 40.

If the review has no title, omit it from the entry.

> Tappin, Nigel. Rev. of *Murder on the Caronia*, by
> Conrad Allen. *Mystery Review* 11.3 (Spring
> 2003): 15.

If the review is neither signed nor titled, begin the entry with *Rev. of* and alphabetize the entry under the title of the work reviewed.

> Rev. of *Anthology of Danish Literature*, ed. F. J. Billeskov Jansen and P. M. Mitchell. *Times Literary Supplement* 7 July 1972: 785.

As shown in the example above, use an appropriate abbreviation (e.g., *ed., comp., trans.*) for the work of someone other than an author.

Series

Between the name of the publication and the volume number, identify a numbered series with an ordinal suffix (*2nd, 3rd*) followed by the abbreviation *ser.* For publications divided between the original series and a new series, show the series with *os* or *ns*, respectively.

> Hill, Christopher. "Sex, Marriage and the Family in England." *Economic History Review* 2nd ser. 31 (1978): 450-63.
>
> Terry, Richard. "Swift's Use of 'Personate' to Indicate Parody." *Notes and Queries* ns 41.2 (June 1994): 196-98.

NOTE: For a serialized article (one that appears in two or more successive issues of a periodical) see "Serialized Article in a Newspaper or Periodical," page 200.

Special Issue

If you cite one article from a special issue of a journal, you may indicate the nature of this special issue, as shown next:

> Fenton, Matthew McCann. "Katrina's Last Casualty: Truth." *Time*. Spec. Issue of *Time* (2005): 55.

If you cite several articles from the special issue, begin the primary citation with the name of the editor:

> Knauer, Kelly, ed. Spec. Issue of *Time* (2005): 1-122.

Once that entry is established, cross reference each article used in the following manner:

```
Dworzak, Thomas. "Elysian Fields." Photograph.
    Knauer, 56-57.
```

> ■ **NOTE:** See also "Cross References to Works in a Collection,"
> page 193.

Speech or Address, Published

```
Agnew, Karen. "Finding and Supporting Instructors
    in Continuing Education." Address to
    Conference on Continuing Education. Topeka, KS
    26 Apr. 2003. Rpt. in part Continuing
    Education Review 9.2 June 2003: 19-22.
United States. President. "Saluting Those Who
    Serve." 18 Jan. 2005. Rpt. in Weekly
    Compilation of Presidential Documents pd24ja05
    txt-10 (21 Jan. 2005): 71-72.
```

Title of the Article

Show the title within quotation marks followed by a period inside the closing quotation marks:

```
Tresemer, Lila Sophia. "The Magdalene Mystique: Why
    Her Archetype Matters." Utne (Nov./Dec. 2005):
    63-64.
```

Title, Omitted

```
Jeffries, Miriam. Oakleaf Journal of Conservation
    30.3 (2003): 393-95.
```

Title, Quotation within the Article's Title

```
Gatta, John J. "The Scarlet Letter as Pre-text for
    Flannery O'Connor's 'Good Country People.'"
    Nathaniel Hawthorne Review 16 (1990): 6-9.
```

Title, within the Article's Title

```
Cornils, Ingo. "The Martians Are Coming! War,
     Peace, Love, and Scientific Progress in H. G.
     Wells's The War of the Worlds and Kurd
     Labwitz's Auf Zwei Planeten." Comparative
     Literature 55.1 (Winter 2003): 24-41.
```

Title, Foreign

```
Correa, Armando, and Maria Morales. "La Importancia
     De Ser." People En Espanol Diciembre/Enero
     2006: 136-41.
```

NOTE: See also "Title of a Book in Another Language," page 201.

Volume, Issue, and Page Numbers for Journals

Most journals are paged continuously through all issues of an entire year, so listing the month of publication is unnecessary. For example, page numbers and a volume number are sufficient for you to find an article in *Eighteenth Century Studies* or *English Literary Renaissance*. However, some journals have separate pagination for each issue. If that is the case, you will need to add an issue number following the volume number, separated by a period:

```
Loranc, Roman. "Remnant Beauty." Lens Work 61
     (Nov./Dec. 2005): 45-61.
```

Add the month also to ease the search for the article: "20.5 (Nov. 2005): 4–12."

11d Bibliography Form—Newspapers

Provide the name of the author; the title of the article; the name of the newspaper as it appears on the masthead, omitting any introductory article (e.g., *Wall Street Journal*, not *The Wall Street Journal*); and the complete date—day, month (abbreviated), and year. Omit any volume and issue numbers.

Provide a page number as listed (e.g., 21, B-7, 13C, D4). For example, *USA Today* uses "6A" but the *New York Times* uses "A6." There is no uniformity among newspapers on this matter, so list the page accurately as an aid to your reader. If the article is not printed on consecutive pages (for example, if it begins on page 1 and skips to page 8), write the first page number and a plus (+) sign (see the entry below).

Newspaper in One Section

Whitfield, Jeffery. "Bracing for Black Friday."
    Clayton News Daily 24 Nov. 2005: 1 + .

Newspaper with Lettered Sections

Long, Bryan. "Building Brings Credibility to
    Projects Office Segment." *Atlanta Business
    Chronicle* 25 Nov. 2005: 3A + .

Newspaper with Numbered Sections

Berger, Susan. "Animal Rescuers, Officials Clash."
    Chicago Tribune 26 Nov. 2005, sec. 1: 1.

Newspaper Editorial with No Author Listed

"New Ballparks Sporting Lots of Empty Seats."
    Editorial. *Atlanta Business Chronicle* 30 May
    2003: 32A.

Newspaper Column, Cartoon, Comic Strip, or Advertisement

Add a description to the entry to explain that the citation refers to something other than a regular news story.

Donlan, Thomas G. "Fine Tuning." Column. *Barron's*
    26 May 2003: 31.

Newspaper Article with City Added

In the case of locally published newspapers, add the city in square brackets (see also the sample entry immediately above).

Hamlin, Emily. "Famalies Grieve for Sons Killed in
    Iraq." *Leaf Chronicle* [Clarksville, TN] 26
    Nov. 2005: A1.

Newspaper Edition or Section

When the masthead lists an edition, add a comma after the date and name the edition (*late ed.*, *city ed.*), followed by a colon and then the page number.

```
Dillon, Sam. "Students Ace State Tests, but Earn
     D's from U.S." New York Times 26 Nov. 2005,
     national ed.: A1 + .
```

Newspaper in a Foreign Language

```
"Les Grands de ce monde reunis a Saint-
     Petersbourg." Le Monde 30 mai 2003: 1.
```

11e Bibliography Form—Government Documents

Since the nature of public documents is so varied, the form of the entry cannot be standardized. Therefore, you should provide sufficient information so that the reader can easily locate the reference. As a general rule, place information in the bibliographic entry in this order (but see below if you know the author, editor, or compiler of the document):

Government

Body or agency

Subsidiary body

Title of document

Identifying numbers

Publication facts

When you cite two or more works by the same government, substitute three hyphens for the name of each government or body that you repeat:

United States. Cong. House.

---. ---. Senate.

---. Dept. of Justice.

Begin with the author's name if known, especially if you cited the name in your text.

Poore, Benjamin Perley, comp. *A Descriptive Catalogue of the Government Publications of the United States, September 5, 1774-March 4, 1881*. US 48th Cong., 2nd sess. Misc. Doc. 67. Washington: GPO, 1885.

Congressional Papers

Senate and House sections are identified by an S or an H with document numbers (e.g., S. Res. 16) and page numbers (e.g., H2345-47).

United States. Cong. Senate. Subcommittee on Juvenile Justice of the Committee on the Judiciary. *Juvenile Justice: A New Focus on Prevention*. 102nd Cong., 2nd sess. S. Hearing 102-1045. Washington, DC: GPO, 1992.
---. ---. ---. *Violent Crime Control Act 1991*. 102d Cong., 1st sess. S. 1241. Washington, DC: GPO, 1991.

If you provide a citation to the *Congressional Record*, you should abbreviate it and provide only the date and page numbers.

Cong. Rec. 18 Nov. 2005: S13285-87.

Executive Branch Documents

United States. Dept. of State. *Foreign Relations of the United States: Diplomatic Papers, 1943*. 5 vols. Washington, DC: GPO, 1943-44.
---. President. *2005 Economic Report of the President*. Washington, DC: GPO, 2005.

Documents of State Governments

Publication information on state papers will vary widely, so provide sufficient data for your reader to find the document.

2004-2005 Statistical Report. Nashville: Tennessee Board of Regents, 2005. TBR A-001-03.

Tennessee Election Returns, 1796–1825. Microfilm.
    Nashville: Tennessee State Library and
    Archives, n.d. M-Film JK 5292 T46.
"Giles County." *2005–06 Directory of Public Schools*.
    Nashville: State Dept. of Educ., n.d. 61.

Legal Citations and Public Statutes

Use the following examples as guidelines for developing your citations, which can usually appear as parenthetical citations in your text, but not on the Works Cited page.

Illinois. Revised Statutes Annotated. Sec. 16-7-81.
    2005.
Noise Control Act of 1972. Pub. L. 92-574. 1972.
    Stat. 86.
People v. McIntosh. California 321 P.3d 876,
    2001-6. 1970.
State v. Lane. Minnesota 263 N. W. 608. 1935.
U.S. Const. Art 2, sec. 1.

11f Electronic Sources (Internet, E-mail, Databases)

Modern technology makes it possible for you to have access to information at your computer. In particular, the Internet opens a cornucopia of information from millions of sources. Other electronic sources include e-mail and databases.

Citing Sources Found on the Internet

Include these items as appropriate to the source:

1. Author/editor name
2. Title of the article within quotation marks, or the title of a posting to a discussion list or forum followed by the words *online posting*, followed by a period.
3. If the document has a printed version, provide the publication information and the date.
4. Information on the electronic publication, such as the title of the site, the date of the posting, and the sponsoring organization.

5. Date of your access, not followed by a comma or period.

6. URL (Uniform Resource Locator), within angle brackets, followed by a period. If you must divide a URL at the end of a line, break it only after a slash.

NOTE: For discussion of the Internet's special format, see pages 58–59. For making judgments about the validity of Internet sources, see pages 50–51.

NOTE: Do not include page numbers unless the Internet article shows original page numbers from the printed version of the journal or magazine. Do not include the total number of paragraphs nor specific paragraph numbers unless the original Internet article has provided them.

World Wide Web Sites

Titles of books and journals may be shown either in italics or with underlining. They are shown in this section with italics.

Abstract

Gellis, Les A., et al. "Socioeconomic Status and Insomnia." *Journal of Abnormal Psychology* 114 (2005). Abstract. 10 Nov. 2005 <http://www.apa.org/journals/features/abn1141111.pdf>.

Advertisement

The Mercado. "Titanic: The Exhibition." *Advertisement.* 2006. 14 Feb. 2006 <http://www.titanicshipofdreams.com/>.

Anonymous Article

"What's Your PSI? Test Your Tire Safety Knowledge." *National Highway Traffic Safety Administration.* n.d. 31 Jan. 2006 <http://www.safercar.gov/Tires/pages/PSI.htm>.

Archive or Scholarly Project

British Poetry Archive. Ed. Jerome McGann and David
        Seaman. 2006. U of Virginia Lib. 19 Apr. 2006
        <http://etext.lib.virginia.edu/britpo.html>.

Article from an Online Magazine

"Controlling Anger—Before It Controls You. APA
        Online. 10 May 2006. <http://www.apa.org/
        pubinfo/anger.html>.

Article from a Scholarly Journal

Bogart, L. M., et al. "Effects of Early and Later
        Marriage on Women's Alcohol Use in Young
        Adulthood: A Prospective Analysis." Journal of
        Studies on Alcohol 66 (2005): 729-37. 22 Mar.
        2006 <http://www.rci.rutgers.edu/~cas2/
        journal/march03/>.

Article Written for the Internet

"History of Elba." Elba on line. 12 Apr. 2006
        <http://www.elba-on-line.com/Informazioni/
        storiaeng.html>.

Audio Program Online   See "Television or Radio Program," page
224.

Cartoon

Parker, Brant. "My Son, the King." Cartoon. Wizard
        of Id. 11 May 2003. 29 Oct. 2005 <http://
        umweb2.unitedmedia.com/ creators/wizardofid/
        archive/wizardofid-20030511.html>.

Chapter or Portion of a Book   Add the name of the chapter after the
author's name:

Dewey, John. "Waste in Education." *The School and*
    Society. Chicago: U of Chicago P, 1907. 4 Feb.
    2006 <http://spartan.ac.brocku.ca/~lward/
    dewey/Dewey_1907/Dewey_1907c.html>.

Article at a Library's Online Service with a Listed URL Most libraries have converted their computer searches to online databases, such as Lexis-Nexis, ProQuest Direct, EBSCOhost, Electric Library, InfoTrac, and others. If the source provides the URL, omit the identifying numbers for the database or the keyword used in the search and include the URL. Here's an example from *InfoTrac*:

Lee, Catherine C. "The South in Toni Morrison's
    Song of Solomon: Initiation, Healing, and
    Home." *Studies in the Literary Imagination* 31
    (1998): 109–23. Abstract. 19 Sept. 2005
    <http://firstsearch.oclc.org/next=NEXTCMD>.

You will know the database is online when you see the full URL at the top or bottom of the printout.

Article from an Online Service to which You Personally Subscribe Many students research topics from their homes, where they use such services as American Online or Netscape. If the URL is provided, use the form of this next example, which is the same as that described immediately above.

Sloan, T. A. "Pilates: Your Ticket to a Longer,
    Leaner You." *Discovery Health* 23 Jan. 2006
    <http://health.discovery.com/centers/
    nutritionfitness/fitness/articles/techniques/
    pilates/pilates.html>.

Article from an Online Service with an Unlisted or Scrambled URL If you access the site by using a keyword, provide a citation that gives the name of the service, the date of access, and the keyword:

Esslin, Martin. "Theater of the Absurd." *Grolier*
    Multimedia Encyclopedia. 2005 ed. Netscape. 22
    Aug. 2005. Keyword: Theater of the Absurd.

Article at a Library's Online Service with no URL listed   On rare occasions you may access online material in the library that has no URL or the URL on your printout is scrambled or incomplete. In such a case, make a citation to the source, then give the name of the database, underlined (if known); the name of the service; the library; and the date of access. If you can easily locate the URL of the service's home page, provide it in angle brackets after your date of access.

> Brezina, Timothy. "Teenage Violence toward
>   Parents as an Adaptation to Family Strain:
>   Evidence from a National Survey of Male
>   Adolescents." *Youth and Society* 30 (1999):
>   416-44. *MasterFILE Elite*. EBSCOhost.
>   Clarksville Montgomery County Library,
>   Clarksville, TN. 23 Feb. 2006 <http://
>   www.ebsco.com>.

E-mail

> Wright, Ellen. "Online Composition Courses." E-mail
>   to the author. 24 Mar. 2006.

Encyclopedia Article Online

> "Kurt Vonnegut, Jr." Online Vers. 2005. *Encarta
>   Encyclopedia*. Online Vers. 2005. 19 Nov. 2005
>   <http://encarta.msn.com/encyclopedia_761572520/
>   Kurt_Vonnegut.html>.

ERIC Database   Be sure to give the URL even if the ERIC identifying numbers are available (see also "Database Online," page 229).

> "America's Children: Key National Indicators of
>   Well-Being." Federal Interagency Forum on
>   Child and Family Statistics. 2003. ERIC
>   ED427897. 18 Sept. 2005 <http://www.goarch.
>   org/goa/departments/gotel/
>   online_videos.html#LIGHT>.

Film, Video, or Film Clip Online

"Epiphany: Festival of Lights." *The History of the
Orthodox Christian Church.* 2005. GoTelecom
Online. 24 Oct. 2005 <http://www.goarch.org/
en/multimedia/video/>.

FTP, TELNET, and GOPHER Sites   Most ftp, telnet, and gopher sites are now found on the World Wide Web:

"Modern Irish Language and Culture Internet FTP
Site." Ed. Lisa L. Spangenberg. 20 Jan. 2004.
3 Oct. 2005 <http://www.digitalmedievalist.com/
urls/irish.html>.

Home Page for an Academic Course

Wilkins, John, Shelley Palmer, and Tom Barrett.
Writing and Speaking about Physics and
Astronomy. Winter 2006. Dept. of Physics, Ohio
State U. 22 Mar. 2006. 2 Apr. 2006
<http://physics.ohio-state.edu/~wilkins/
writing/>.

Home Page for an Academic Department

Department of Humanities. Dept. home page. Clayton
State U. 3 Dec. 2005. 12 Dec. 2005 <http://
a-s.clayton.edu/humanities/>.

Home Page for an Academic Site   Since you are not citing a specific article, you can refer to home pages in your text, but not in the bibliography.

Robert Penn Warren: 1905-1989. 2 Apr. 2006
<http://www.english.uiuc.edu/maps/poets/s_z/
warren/warren.htm>.

Home Page for a Personal Web Site

Nguyen, Xyin Trin. Home Page. 22 Nov. 2005. 2 Apr.
2006 <http://www.nmt.edu/~xtnguyen>.

Interview

Strassman, Marc. "Is Journalism Dead?" Interview
with Pete Hamill, author of *News Is a Verb*.
Strassman Files. *BookRadio* 1998. 24 Nov. 2005
<http://www.bookradio.com/>.

Journal Article

Paap, Chris, and Douglas Raybeck. "A Differently
Gendered Landscape: Gender and Agency in the
Web-based Personals." *Electronic Journal of
Sociology*. (2005). 22 Jan. 2006 <http://
www.sociology.org/content/2005/tier2/
paap__genderedlandscape.pdf>.

Letter

Peck, Ray. "Politics Played with Schools." Letter
to the Editor. *The Billings Outpost Online* 24
Nov. 2005. 28 Nov. 2005 <http://www.
billingsnews.com/
story?storyid=18562&issue295>.

Linkage Data (An Accessed File)

"What Happens to Recycled Plastics?" Online
posting. Lkd. Better World Discussion Topics
at Recycling Discussion Group nd. 18 Mar. 2006
<http://www.betterworld.com/BWZ/9602/
learn.htm>.

Magazine Article Online

Weintraub, Arlene. "Gene Therapy is Respectable
Again." *BusinessWeek Online* 23 Nov. 2005. 2
Dec. 2005 <http://www.businessweek.com/
technology/content/nov2005/
tc20051123_355639.htm>.

Manuscript

Girondo, Oliverio. *Scarecrow & Other Anomilies.*
Trans. Gilbert Alter-Gilbert. Manuscript, 2002.
24 Aug. 2005 <http://www.xenosbooks.com/
scarecrow.html>.

Map

"Virginia—1785." Map. *U.S. County Formation Maps
1643-Present.* Genealogy, Inc. 1999. 24 Sept.
2005 <http://www.segenealogy.com/virginia/
va_maps/va_cf.htm>.

MOO, MUD, & Other Chat Rooms

"Virtual Conference on Mary Shelley's *The Last
Man.*" Villa Diodati at EmoryMOO. 13 Sept.
1997. 28 Oct. 2004 <http://www.rc.umd.edu/
villa/vc97/Shelley_9_13_97.html>.

Chat rooms seldom have great value, but on occasion you might find
something that you wish to cite; if so, use this form:

"Weight Loss Support." 30 May 2006. *Yahoo! Chat.* 30
May 2006 <http://chat.yahoo.com/?room=
Weight%20Loss%20Support%3A1%3A%3A1602757662
&identity=jfuller22&client=DHTML>.

Newsgroup, Usenet News, Forum

Kalb, Jim. "Conservatism FAQ." Online Posting. 1
May 2004. Political Newsgroup. 13 Oct. 2005
<http://www.faqs.org/faqs/conservatism/faq/>.

Add additional data to cite a document that has been forwarded.

Kalb, Jim. "Conservatism FAQ." 1 June 2003. Fwd. by
Gwen Everett. Online posting. 12 June 2003.
Environment Newsgroup. 13 June 2003 <http://
nwww.faqs.org/faqs/conservatism/faq/>.

Newsletter

```
"Job Market Poised to Expand." MSU News Bulletin
     37.7 (23 Nov. 2005). 28 Nov. 2005 <http://
     www.newsbulletin.msu.edu/nov2305/
     career_trends.html>.
```

Newspaper Article, Column, Editorial

```
Lowenthal, Alena. "Thank Goodness! We've Got Some
     Alternatives to the Mall." 25 Nov. 2005. 28
     Nov. 2005 <http://www.miami.com/mld/
     miamiherald/living/13248839.htm>.
```

Novel

```
Lawrence, D. H. "Chapter 1." Lady Chatterly's
     Lover. 1928. 26 Sept. 2005 <http://
     bibliomania.com/fiction/dhl/chat/chat1.html>.
```

Online Posting for E-mail Discussion Groups   List the Internet
site if known; otherwise show the e-mail address of the list's moderator.

```
Chapman, David. "An Electoral System for Iraq."
     Online Posting. 21 June 2005. Democracy Design
     Forum. 27 Jan. 2006 <http://www.
     democdesignforum.demon.co.uk/ESforIraq060704.
     htm>.
Chapman, David. "An Electoral System for Iraq."
     Online Posting. 21 June 2005. Democracy Design
     Forum. 27 Jan. 2006 <chapman@democdesignforum.
     demon.co.uk>.
```

Photo, Painting, Sculpture   MLA style does not require you to label
the type of work, as shown in the first example of a photograph. Usually,
the text will have established the nature of the work. However, if you feel
that clarification is necessary, as in the case of "The Blessed Damozel,"
which is both a painting and a poem, you may wish to designate the form.

```
Farrar, Ray. "Leadenhall Market." 12 Jan. 2006 <http://
     www.jrfarrar.fsnet.co.uk/lon1/image17.htm>.
```

Rossetti, Dante. "The Blessed Damozel." 1875-78.
  Painting. *Rossetti Archive*. 30 Sept. 2005
  <http://www.rossettiarchive.org/docs/
  1-1847.s244.raw.html>.
"Leaping Gazelle, 1936." Bronze Sculpture. Marshall
  M. Fredericks Sculpture Museum. 2001. 29 Aug.
  2005 <http://www.svsu.edu/mfsm/
  collections.htm>.

Poem, Song, or Story

Dylan, Bob. "Tangled Up in Blue." Song lyrics. 13
  Mar. 2005. <http://bobdylan.com/songs/tangled.
  html>.
Hardy, Thomas. "To a Lady." *Wessex Poems and Other
  Verses*. 1898. *Project Bartleby*. 2005 Great
  Books Online. 10 Jan. 2006
  <http://www.bartleby.com/121/40.html>.

Report

"Pharmacy Benefit Managers: Ownership of Mail-Order
  Pharmacies: A Federal Trade Commission
  Report." Federal Trade Commission. Aug. 2005.
  4 Dec. 2005 <http://www.ftc.gov/reports/
  pharmbenefit05/050906pharmbenefitrpt.pdf>.

Serialized Article

Frank, Laura. "Worker: 'I Didn't Get That at Home."
  Tennessean.com 9 Feb. 1997. Pt. 1 of a series,
  An Investigation into Illnesses around the
  Nation's Nuclear Weapons Sites, begun 9 Feb.
  1997. 20 Oct. 2005 <http://www.tennessean.com/
  special/ oakridge/part1/frames/html>.
Thomas, Susan. "Oak Ridge Workers Offered Medical
  Screening." *Tennessean.com* 21 Jan. 1999. Pt. 2
  of a series, An Investigation into Illnesses
  around the Nation's Nuclear Weapons Sites,
  begun 9 Feb. 1997. 20 Oct. 2005 <http://
  www.tennessean.com/special/oakridge/part2/
  frames/html>.

Thomas, Susan, Laura Frank, and Anne Paine. "Taking the Poison." *Tennessean.com* 9 Feb. 1997. Pt. 3 of a series, An Investigation into Illnesses around the Nation's Nuclear Weapons Sites, begun 9 Feb. 1997. 20 Oct. 2005 <http://www.tennessean.com/special/oakridge/part3/frames/html>.

Song   See "Poem, Song, or Story," page 223.

Sound Clip, Speech, or Recording   See "Television or Radio Program," page 224.

Story   See "Poem, Song, or Story," page 223.

Synchronous Communication   See "Moo, Mud, and Other Chat Rooms," page 221.

Television or Radio Program

Gross, Terry. "Roseanne Cash Remembers Her Father, Johnny." *Fresh Air*. NPR Online. 25 Nov. 2005. Audio transcript. 29 Nov. 2005 <http://www.npr.org/templates/story/story.php?storyId = 5027605>.

University Posting, Online Article

Guinane, Pat. "Uncle Sam's Pocket." Online Posting. Nov. 2005. U of Illinois at Springfield. 6 Dec. 2005 <http://illinoisissues.uis.edu/features/2005nov/federal.html>.

Video   See "Film, Video, or Film Clip," page 219.

Web Site, General Reference   As long as you are not citing a specific article but merely making reference to a site, provide the address in your text, *not* on the Works Cited page.

Further information about this program can be found
    at the Web site for the Department of Psychology
    at the University of Wisconsin-Parkside
    <http://www.uwp.edu/academic/psychology>.

Working Papers

Deighton, John. "The Presentation of Self in the
    Information Age." Working Paper #04-059,
    Harvard Business School, 2004-2005. 30 Jan.
    2006 <http://www.hbs.edu/units/marketing/
    research.htm>.

11g Citing Sources Found on CD-ROM

CD-ROM technology provides information in four different ways, and
each method of transmission requires an adjustment in the form of the
entry for your works cited page.

Full-Text Articles with Publication Information for the Printed Source

Full-text articles are available from national distributors, such as Information Access Company (InfoTrac), UMI-Proquest (Proquest), Silverplatter, or SIRS CD-ROM Information Systems. (Note: Most of these sources are also available online.) Conform to the examples that follow:

DePalma, Antony. "Mexicans Renew Their Pact on the
    Economy, Retaining the Emphasis on Stability."
    New York Times 25 Sept. 1994: 4. New York
    Times Ondisc. CD-ROM. UMI-Proquest. Jan. 2005.
Mann, Thomas E., and Norman J. Ornstein.
    "Shipshape? A Progress Report on Congressional
    Reform." Brookings Review Spring 1994: 40-45.
    SIRS Researcher. CD-ROM. Boca Raton: SIRS,
    1994. Art. 57.

■ NOTE: See also page 205 for citing SIRS in its loose-leaf
form.

■ **HINT:** Complete information may not be readily available—
for example, the original publication data may be missing.
In such cases, provide what is available:

Silver, Daniel J. "The Battle of the Books." Rev.
of *The Western Canon: The Books and School of
the Ages*, by Harold Bloom. *Resource/One*.
CD-ROM. UMI-ProQuest. Feb. 2005.

Full-Text Articles with No Publication Information for a Printed Source

Sometimes the original printed source of an article or report will not be
provided by the distributor of the CD-ROM database. In such a case, conform to the examples that follow, which provide limited data:

"Faulkner Biography." *Discovering Authors*. CD-ROM.
Detroit: Gale, 2001.
"U.S. Population by Age: Urban and Urbanized Areas."
1999 U.S. Census of Population and Housing.
CD-ROM. US Bureau of the Census. 2000.

Complete Books and Other Publications on CD-ROM

Cite this type of source as you would a book, and then provide information to the electronic source that you accessed.

The Bible. Life Application Study Bible. CD-ROM.
Carol Stream, IL: Tyndale House, 2005.
English Poetry Full-Text Database. Re. 2. CD-ROM.
Cambridge, Eng.: Chadwyck, 2003.
"John F. Kennedy." *InfoPedia*. CD-ROM. N.p.: Future
Vision, n.d.
Poe, Edgar Allan. "Fall of the House of Usher."
Electronic Classical Library. CD-ROM. Garden
Grove, CA: World Library, 1999.
Chaucer, Geoffrey. "The Wife of Bath's Tale."
Canterbury Tales. CD-ROM facsimile text.
Princeton: Films for the Humanities and
Sciences, 2000.

Abstracts to Books and Articles Provided by the National Distributors

As a service to readers, the national distributors have members of their staff write abstracts of articles and books if the original authors have not provided such abstracts. As a result, an abstract that you find on Info-Trac and ProQuest may not be written by the original author, so you should not quote such abstracts. You may quote from abstracts that say, "Abstract written by the author." Silverplatter databases *do* have abstracts written by the original authors. In either case, you need to show in the works cited entry that you have cited from the abstract, so conform to the example that follows, which provides name, title, publication information, the word *abstract*, the name of the database italicized, the medium (CD-ROM), the name of the vender, and—if available to you—the electronic publication date (month and year).

Figueredo, Aurelio J., and Laura Ann McCloskey.
    "Sex, Money, and Paternity: The Evolutionary
    Psychology of Domestic Violence." *Ethnology
    and Sociobiology* 14 (1993): 353-79. Abstract.
    PsycLIT. CD-ROM. Silverplatter. 12 Jan. 2003.

Nonperiodical Publication on CD-ROM, Diskette, or Magnetic Tape

Cite a CD-ROM, diskette, or magnetic tape as you would for a book with the addition of a descriptive word. If relevant, show edition (3rd ed.), release (Rel. 2), or version (Ver. 3). Conform to the examples that follow:

Lester, James D. *Introduction to Greek Mythology:
    Computer Slide Show.* 12 lessons on CD-ROM.
    Clarksville, TN: Austin Peay State U, 2005.
"Nuclear Medicine Technologist." *Guidance
    Information System.* 17th ed. Diskette.
    Cambridge: Riverside-Houghton, 1992.
*Statistics on Child Abuse—Montgomery County,
    Tennessee.* Rel. 2. Magnetic tape.
    Clarksville, TN: Harriett Cohn Mental Health
    Center, 2006.

Encyclopedia Article

For an encyclopedia article on a compact diskette, use the following form:

> "Abolitionist Movement." *Compton's Interactive*
> *Encyclopedia*. CD-ROM. The Learning Company,
> 2006.

Multidisc Publication

When citing a multidisc publication, follow the term *CD-ROM* with the total number of discs or with the disc that you cited from:

> *Parsees 2.0: Interactive Sources and Studies on*
> *Ancient Greece*. CD-ROM. Disc 3. New Haven:
> Yale UP, 2000.

11h Other Electronic Sources

Citing a Source That You Access in More Than One Medium

Some distributors issue packages that include different media, such as CD-ROM and accompanying microfiche or a diskette and an accompanying videotape. Cite such publications as you would a nonperiodical CD-ROM (see item 3 above) with the addition of the media available with this product.

> Franking, Holly. *The Martensville Nightmare*. Vers.
> 1.0. Diskette, CD-ROM. Prairie Village:
> Diskotech, 2005.
> Jolly, Peggy. "A Question of Style." *Exercise*
> *Exchange* 26.2 (1982): 39–40. *ERIC*. CD-ROM,
> microfiche. Silverplatter. Feb. 17, 1995.
> ED236601, fiche 1.
> Silver, Daniel J. "The Battle of the Books." Rev. of
> *The Western Canon: The Books and School of the*
> *Ages*, by Harold Bloom. *Resource/One*. CD-ROM,
> microfiche S-637. UMI-Proquest. Feb. 1995.
> Chaucer, Geoffrey. "Prologue." *Canterbury Tales*.
> Videocassette, CD-ROM facsimile text.
> Princeton: Films for the Humanities and
> Sciences, 2005.

Citing a Source Found on an Online Database

To cite an online database, such as DIALOG, conform to the style shown in these samples:

> Bronner, E. "Souter Voices Concern over Abortion
>   Curb." *Boston Globe* 31 Oct. 1990: 1. Online.
>   Dialog. 22 Nov. 1997.
> Priest, Patricia Joyner. "Self-Disclosure on
>   Television: The Counter-Hegemonic Struggle of
>   Marginalized Groups on 'Donahue.'" Diss. New
>   York U, 1990. *DAI* 53.7 (1993): 2147A.
>   *Dissertation Abstracts Online.* Online. Dialog.
>   10 Feb. 1994.

Material Accessed through E-mail

Electronic mail may be treated as a letter or memo (see page 233). Provide the name of the sender, a title or subject if one is listed, a description of the mail (e.g., "E-mail to Greg Norman"), and the date of transmission.

> Ramirez, Margo. "Dorm Supervisors Check-in
>   Checklist." E-mail to Humes users. 18 Aug.
>   2005.
> James, Tominka. E-mail to the author. 16 May 2006.

11i Bibliography Form — Other Sources

Advertisement

Provide the title of the advertisement, within quotation marks, or the name of the product or company, not within quotation marks, the label *Advertisement*, and publication information.

> "Southern Women Writers Conference." Advertisement.
>   *Oxford American* Summer 2005: 111.
> OnStar. Advertisement. CNNLive. 4 Aug. 2005.
> Carmax. Billboard advertisement. Stockbridge, GA.
>   Jan. 2006.

Artwork

If you actually experience the work itself, use the form shown by the next two entries:

Remington, Frederic. *Mountain Man*. Metropolitan
    Museum of Art, New York.
Wyeth, Andrew. *Hay Ledge*. Private Collection of Mr.
    and Mrs. Joseph E. Levine.

If the art work is a special showing at a museum, use the form of this next example.

Michals, Duane. "The Last Rose of Summer."
    Pace/Macgill Gallery, New York. 3 Dec. 2005.
"Oscar Bluemner: A Passion for Color." Whitney
    Museum of American Art, New York. 10 Feb.
    2006.

Use this next form to cite reproductions in books and journals.

Lee-Smith, Hughie. *Temptation*. 1991. *A History of
    African-American Artists: From 1792 to the
    Present*. Ed. Romare Bearden and Harry
    Henderson. New York: Pantheon, 1993.
Raphael. *School of Athens*. The Vatican, Rome. *The
    World Book-Encyclopedia*. 2005 ed.

If you show the date of the original, place the date immediately after the title.

Raphael. *School of Athens*. 1510-1511. The Vatican,
    Rome. *The World Book-Encyclopedia*. 2005 ed.

Broadcast Interview

Gray, Jim. "NBA Coaching Vacancies." Interview.
    ESPN. 4 June 2005.

Bulletin

The South Carolina Market Bulletin. Columbia, SC:
    South Carolina Department of Agriculture, 15
    May, 2005.

Maryland State Bar Association's Public Awareness
    Committee. *Appointing a Guardian*. Baltimore:
    Maryland State Bar Association. 2005.

Cartoon

If you cannot decipher the name of the cartoonist and cannot find a title, use this form:

Cartoon. *Reminisce* July/Aug. 2005: 60.

Sometimes you will have the artist's name but not the name of the cartoon:

Artley, Bob. Cartoon. *Reminisce* July/Aug. 2005: 52.

Some cartoons are reprinted in magazines:

Ramirez. "Peace." Cartoon. Rpt. in *The Weekly
    Standard* 2 June, 2005: 13.

Computer Software

Publisher Deluxe 2003. Redmond, WA: Microsoft, 2003.

Conference Proceedings

Alejna Brugos, Manuella R. Clark-Cotton, and
    Seungwan Ha, eds. *BUCLD-29: Proceedings of the
    Twenty-ninth Boston University Conference on
    Language Development*. Apr. 2005. Somerville,
    MA: Cascadilla, 2005.

Dissertation, Published

Nordstrand, Thomas. *Basic Testing and Strength
    Design of Corrugated Board and Containers*.
    Diss. Lund U, 2003. Stockholm: EFI, 2003.

Dissertation, Unpublished

Patel-McCune, Santha. "An Analysis of Homophone
    Errors in the Writing of 7th Grade Language
    Arts Students: Implications for Middle School
    Teachers." Diss. Southern Tech. U, 2006.

> ■ **NOTE:** If you cite only the abstract of a dissertation, see "Abstract in an Abstracts Journal," page 204 for the correct form.

Film, Videocassette, or DVD

Cite the title of a film, the director, the distributor, and the year.

> *Harry Potter and the Goblet of Fire*. Dir. Mike Newell. Warner Bros. Video, 2005.

If relevant to your study, add the names of performers, writers, or producers after the name of the director.

> *The Passion of the Christ*. Dir. Mel Gibson. Screenplay by Benedict Fitzgerald and Mel Gibson. Newmarket, 2004.

If the film is a DVD, videocassette, filmstrip, slide program, or videodisc, add the type of medium before the name of the distributor. Add the date of the original film, if relevant, before the name of the medium.

> Citizen Kane. Dir. Orson Welles. 1941. DVD. Warner, 2002.

> Crimmins, Morton. "Robert Lowell—American Poet." Lecture. Videocassette. Western State U, 2005.

If you are citing the accomplishments of the director or a performer, begin the citation with that person's name.

> Mangold, James, dir. *Walk the Line*. Perf. Joaquin Phoenix and Reese Witherspoon. Sony, 2005.

If you cannot find certain information, such as the original date of the film, cite what is available.

> Altman, Robert, dir. *The Room*. Perf. Julian Sands, Linda Hunt, Annie Lennox. Videocassette. Prism.

Interview, Unpublished

For an interview that you conduct, name the person interviewed, the type of interview (e.g., telephone interview, personal interview, e-mail interview), and the date.

Carter, Emma. "Growing Georgia Greens." Telephone
interview. 5 Mar. 2005.

See also "Published Interview," page 205, and "Broadcast Interview,"
page 230.

Letter, Personal

Knight, Charles. Letter to the author. 21 Jan. 2006.

Letter, Published

Eisenhower, Dwight. Letter to Richard Nixon. 20
April 1968. *Memoirs of Richard Nixon*. By
Richard Nixon. New York: Grosset, 1978.

Loose-leaf Collections

If you cite an article from *SIRS*, *Opposing Viewpoints*, or other loose-
leaf collections, provide both the original publication data and then add
information for the loose-leaf volume, as shown in this next example:

"The Human Genetic Code." Illustration. Facts on
File 29 June 2000: 437-38.
Hodge, Paul. "The Andromeda Galaxy." *Mercury*
July/Aug. 1993: 98 + . *Physical Science*. Ed.
Eleanor Goldstein. Vol. 2. Boca Raton: SIRS,
1994. Art. 24.
Cox, Rachel S. "Protecting the National Parks." *CQ*
Researcher 16 July 2000: 523 + . Washington,
DC: Congressional Quarterly Inc., 2000.

Manuscripts (ms.) and Typescripts (ts.)

Glass, Malcolm. Journal 3, ms. M. Glass Private
Papers, Clarksville, TN.
Tanner. Ms. 346. Bodleian Library, Oxford, Eng.
Williams, Ralph. Notebook 15, ts. Williams Papers.
Vanderbilt U., Nashville.

Map

Treat a map as you would an anonymous work, but add a descriptive
label, such as *map*, *chart*, *survey*, unless the title describes the medium.

County Boundaries and Names. United States Base Map
GE=50, No. 86. Washington, DC: GPO, 2005.
Pennsylvania. Map. Chicago: Rand, 2006.

Microfilm or Microfiche

Chapman, Dan. "Panel Could Help Protect Children."
Winston-Salem Journal 14 Jan. 1990: 14.
Newsbank: Welfare and Social Problems 12
(1990): fiche 1, grids A8-11.
Jolly, Peggy. "A Question of Style." *Exercise
Exchange* 26.2 (1982): 39-40. *ERIC* ED2336601,
fiche 1.
Tuckerman, H. T. "James Fenimore Cooper."
Microfilm. *North American Review* 89 (1859):
298-316.

Miscellaneous Materials (Program, Leaflet, Poster, Announcement)

"Earth Day." Poster. Louisville. 20 Mar. 2006.
"Spring Family Weekend." Program. Nashville: Fisk
U. 1 Apr. 2006.

Musical Composition

For a musical composition, begin with the composer's name, followed
by a period. Underline or italicize the title of an opera, ballet, or work
of music identified by name, but do not italicize or enclose within quotation marks the form, number, and key when these are used to identify an instrumental composition.

Mozart, Wolfgang A. *Jupiter*. Symphony No. 41.
Wagner, Richard. *Lohengrin*.

Treat a published score as you would a book.

Legrenzi, Giovanni. *La Buscha*. Sonata for
Instruments. *Historical Anthology of Music*.
Ed. Archibald T. Davison and Willi Apel.
Cambridge, MA: Harvard UP, 1950. 70-76.

Pamphlet

Treat pamphlets as you would a book.

> Federal Reserve Board. *Consumer Handbook to Credit*
> *Protection Laws.* Washington, DC: GPO, 2006.
> Westinghouse Advanced Power Systems. *Nuclear Waste*
> *Management: A Manageable Task.* Madison, PA:
> Author, n.d.

Performance

Treat a performance (e.g., play, opera, ballet, or concert) as you would a film, but include the site (normally the theater and city) and the date of the performance.

> *Lakota Sioux Indian Dance Theatre.* Cherokee
> Heritage Center, Tahlequah, OK. 12 May 2005.
> *Much Ado About Nothing.* By William Shakespeare.
> Folger Elizabethan Theatre, Washington, D.C.:
> 29 Oct. 2005.
> *The Abduction of Seraglio.* By Mozart. Chicago Opera
> Theater, Chicago. 3 May 2006.

If your text emphasizes the work of a particular individual, begin with the appropriate name.

> Hoang, Haivan, and Doug Dangler. "Getting to Know
> You: Database Information for Writing
> Centers." Conf. on Coll. Composition and
> Communication Convention. Palmer House Hotel,
> Chicago, 24 March, 2006.
> Prégardien, Christoph. "Winterreise." Alice Tully
> Hall, New York. 11 Dec. 2005.
> Durst, Will, comedian. Zanies, Chicago. 2 Dec.
> 2005.

Public Address or Lecture

Identify the nature of the address (e.g., lecture, reading), include the site (normally the lecture hall and city), and the date of the performance.

```
Irvine, Sherry. "Migration Within the British
     Isles: What Genealogists Need to Know."
     Lecture. St. Louis Genealogical Soc., St.
     Louis. 29 Oct. 2005.
```

Recording on Record, Tape, or Disk

If you are not citing a compact disc, indicate the medium (e.g., audio-cassette, audiotape [reel-to-reel tape], or LP [long-playing record]).

```
"Chaucer: The Nun's Priest's Tale." Canterbury
     Tales. Narr. in Middle English by Alex
     Edmonds. Audiocassette. London, 2005.
Dylan, Bob. "The Times They Are A-Changin'." Bob
     Dylan's Greatest Hits. LP. CBS, 1967.
Reich, Robert B. Locked in the Cabinet: A Political
     Memoir. 4 audiocassettes abridged. New York:
     Random Audio, 1997.
Midler, Bette. "Is That All There Is?" Bette Midler
     Sings the Peggy Lee Songbook. CD. Sony, 2005.
Tchaikovsky. Romeo and Juliet. Fantasy-Overture
     after Shakespeare. New Philharmonia Orchestra
     London. Cond. Lawrence Siegel. DVD. Classical
     Masters, 2000.
```

Do not underscore, italicize, or enclose within quotation marks a private recording or tape. However, you should include the date, if avail-able, as well as the location and the identifying number.

```
Walpert, Wanda A. Folk Stories of the Smokey
     Mountains. Rec. Feb. 1995. Audiotape. U of
     Knoxville. Knoxville, TN. UTF.34.82.
```

Cite a libretto, liner notes, or booklet that accompanies a recording in the form shown in the following example.

```
Nelson, Willie. Booklet. The Great Divide. By
     Willie Nelson. UMG, 2002.
```

Report

Unbound reports are placed within quotation marks; bound reports are treated as books:

Coca-Cola Company. 2005 Annual Report. Atlanta:
   Author, 2005.
Franco, Lynn. "Confidence Slips Amid Fragile
   Economy." Report. The Conference Board. New
   York: CBS/Broadcast Group, 23 Jan. 2006.

Reproductions, Photographs, and Photocopies

Blake, William. *Comus*. Plate 4. Photograph in Irene
   Taylor. "Blake's *Comus* Designs." *Blake Studies*
   4 (Spring 1972): 61.
Michener, James A. "Structure of Earth at
   Centennial, Colorado." Line drawing in
   Centennial. By Michener. New York: Random,
   1974. 26.
Snowden, Mary. *Jersey Pears*. 1982. *American
   Realism: Twentieth Century Drawings and
   Watercolors*. New York: Abrams, 1986. 159.

Table, Illustration, Chart, or Graph

Tables or illustrations of any kind published within works need a detailed
label (chart, table, figure, photograph, and so on):

"Financial Indicators: Money and Interest Rates."
   Table. *Economist* 8 July 2000: 105.
Alphabet. Chart. Columbus: Scholastic, 2006.

Television or Radio Program

If available or relevant, provide information in this order: the episode (in
quotation marks), the title of the program (underscored or italicized),
title of the series (not underscored nor in quotation marks), name of
the network, call letters and city of the local station, and the broadcast
date. Add other information (such as narrator) after the episode or program narrated or directed or performed. Place the number of episodes,
if relevant, before the title of the series.

"Distance Learning Class: The Cable Center at the
   Univ. of Denver." Host: Brian Lamb. *Washington
   Journal*. C-SPAN. 6 June 2003.

The Virgin Queen. By Paula Milne. Perf. Anne-Marie
    Duff. 2 episodes. Masterpiece Theatre. Introd.
    Russell Baker. PBS. WCDN, Nashville. 13 Nov.
    2005.

"Should the 22nd Amendment Be Repealed?" *Crossfire*.
    Hosts James Carvelle, Paul Begala, Tucker
    Carlson, and Bob Novak. CNN. 30 May 2005.

Prairie Home Companion. NPR. WABE, Atlanta. 19 Nov.
    2005.

Thesis

See "Dissertation, Unpublished," page 231.

Transparency

Sharp, La Vaughn, and William E. Loeche. *The
    Patient and Circulatory Disorders: A Guide for
    Instructors*. 54 transparencies, 99 overlays.
    Philadelphia: Lorrenzo, 2005.

Unpublished Paper

Schuler, Wren. "Prufrock and His Cat." Unpublished
    essay, 2005.

Voice Mail

Nerbarger, Henry. "Memo to Lester." Voice mail to
    the author. 6 Jan. 2006.

CHAPTER TWELVE

PREPARING ELECTRONIC RESEARCH PROJECTS

Creating your research paper electronically has a number of advantages:

- *It's easy.* Creating electronic research papers can be as simple as saving a file, and your school probably has resources for publishing your paper electronically.

- *It offers multimedia potential.* Unlike paper documents, electronic documents enable you to include anything available in a digital form—including text, illustrations, sound, and video.

- *It can link your reader to more information.* Your readers can click a hyperlink to access additional sources of information. (A hyperlink or link is a highlighted word or image that, when clicked, lets readers jump from one place to another—for example, from your research paper to a Web site on your subject.)

Before you decide to create your research paper electronically, consider three questions:

1. **What support does your school provide?** Most institutions are making investments in technology and the personnel to support it. Investigate how your college will help you publish in an electronic medium.

2. **Is electronic publishing suitable for your research paper?** Ask yourself what your readers will gain from reading an electronic text rather than the traditional paper version. Will an electronic format really help you get your ideas to readers?

3. **What form will it take?** Electronic research papers appear generally in one of the following forms:
   - A word processed document (see section 12a)
   - An electronic presentation or slide show (see section 12b)
   - A Web site (see section 12c)

12a Using Word Processing to Create Electronic Documents

The easiest way to create an electronic document is by using word processing programs such as Microsoft Word® or Corel WordPerfect® and then distributing your report in its electronic form rather than printing it out. (See Figure 12.1 for an example of how such a research paper might look.)

Most popular word processing programs include tools for handling features such as:

Graphics. Word processors can accommodate graphics in a variety of formats, including .gif and .jpg (see the graphic in Figure 12.1 for an example; see section 12d on page 244 for more information on GIF and JPEG formats).

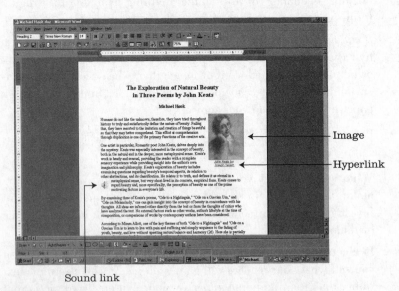

Sound link

■ FIGURE 12.1

Word processed research paper.

Sound and video. Word processors can include several common audio and video clip formats. Usually, the reader has to click on an icon to activate the clip (see the sound link in Figure 12.1).

Hyperlinks. Readers can click to go to a Web site for further reading (see the underlined hyperlink in the text of Figure 12.1).

12b Building a Slide Show

If you plan an oral presentation, an electronic slide show can help illustrate your ideas. Electronic presentations differ from word processed documents in that each page, or slide, constitutes one computer screen. By clicking, you (or another reader) can move to the next slide (see Figure 12.2).

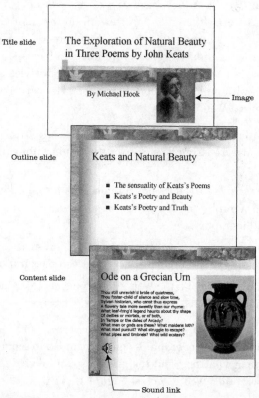

■■■ **FIGURE 12.2**
Research paper slide presentation.

Since each slide can hold only limited information, condense the content of each slide.

12c Creating Pages with Hypertext Markup Language (HTML)

Creating a Web page or a Web site involves collecting or making a series of computer files—some of them the HTML files that contain the basic text and layout for your pages, and others that contain the graphics, sounds, or video that go in your pages.

Using a Web Page Editor to Create Web Pages

The easiest way to create pages is with a Web page editor such as Microsoft FrontPage®, Adobe Page Mill®, or Netscape Composer®. These programs work differently, but they all do the same thing—create Web pages. Using them is like using a word processor: you enter or paste in text, insert graphics or other multimedia objects, and save the file to disk. You can also specify fonts, font sizes, font styles (like bold), alignment, lists with bullets, and numbered lists. Here are a few tips for entering text into a Web page:

- Use bold rather than underlining for emphasis and titles. On a Web site, links are underlined, so any other underlining may cause confusion.

- Do not use tabs. HTML does not support tabs for indenting the first line of a paragraph. You also won't be able to use hanging indents for your bibliography.

- Do not double-space. The Web page editor automatically single-spaces lines of text and double-spaces between paragraphs.

- Make all lines flush left on the Works Cited page; HTML does not support hanging indentions.

When the word processing software converts your document to HTML, it also converts any graphics you've included to separate graphics files. Together, your text and the graphics can be viewed in a Web browser like any other Web page (see Figure 12.3).

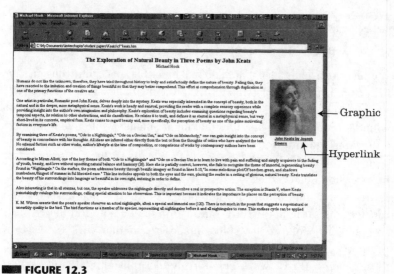

Graphic

Hyperlink

FIGURE 12.3
Single Web page research paper.

Your research paper will look somewhat different in HTML format than in its word processed format. In some ways, HTML is less flexible than word processing, but you can still use word processing software to make changes to your HTML-formatted paper.

> **HINT:** For more information on building Web pages and sites, see the following Web site: NCSA Beginner's Guide to HTML **http://archive.ncsa.uiuc.edu/General/Internet/ WWW/HTMLprimer.html.**

Citing Your Sources in a Web Research Paper

If you are using MLA, APA, or CSE styles, include parenthetical citations in the text itself and create a separate Web page for references. Remember to include such a page in your plans and to provide hyperlinks pointing to it from various places in the paper.

12d Using Graphics in Your Electronic Research Paper

Graphics are usually files that take up a lot of file space, but you can save them as either JPEGs or GIFs to make them smaller. In fact, Web sites can use only graphics saved in these formats. Both formats compress redundant information in a file, making it smaller while retaining most of the image quality. You can recognize the file format by looking at the extension to the file name—GIFs have the extension .gif, and JPEGs have the extension .jpg or .jpeg.

GIF stands for Graphical Interchange Format, which develops and transfers digital images. JPEG stands for Joint Photographic Experts Group, which compresses color images to smaller files for ease of transport.

In general, JPEGs work best for photographs and GIFs work best for line drawings. To save a file as a GIF or JPEG, open it in an image-editing program like Adobe Photoshop® and save the file as one of the two types (for example, keats.jpg or keats.gif).

Programs usually also have menu commands for inserting graphics; refer to your user documentation to find out how to do so.

Creating Your Own Digital Graphics

Making your own graphics file is complex but rewarding. It adds a personal creativity to your research paper. Use one of the following techniques:

- **Use a graphics program,** such as Macromedia Freehand® or Adobe Illustrator®. With such software you can create a graphics file and save it in JPEG or GIF format.

- **Use a scanner** to copy your drawings, graphs, photographs, and other matter. Programs such as Adobe Photoshop® and JASC Paintshop Pro® are useful for modifying scanned photographs.

- **Create original photographs with a digital camera.** Digital cameras usually save images as JPEGs, so you won't need to convert the files into a usable format.

As long as you create JPEG files or GIF files for your graphics, you can transport the entire research paper to a Web site.

12e Delivering Your Electronic Research Paper to Readers

Follow your instructor's requirements for delivering your electronic research paper, or use one of the techniques in the following checklist.

CHECKLIST DELIVERING YOUR ELECTRONIC RESEARCH PAPER

- **Floppy disk.** Floppy disks are a convenient way to share information. However, they are unreliable, and papers with graphics, sound, or video may not fit on a disk.

- **Zip disk.** A Zip disk or other proprietary format holds much larger files than a floppy disk does, but your reader/professor must own a drive that can read it.

- **CD-ROM disks.** These disks hold large amounts of data and thus work well for transmitting graphics, sound, or video files. However, you must own or have access to a CD-R (Compact Disk Recordable) or CD-RW (Compact Disk Recordable/Writable) drive. Most readers have regular CD-ROM drives that can read your disks, but you might want to confirm this beforehand.

- **E-mail.** E-mailing your file as an attachment is the fastest way to deliver your electronic research paper; however, this approach works best if you have a single file, like a word processed research paper, rather than a collection of related files, like a Web site.

- **Web site.** If you've created a Web site or Web page, you can upload your work to a Web server, and readers can access your work on the Internet. Procedures for uploading Web sites vary from school to school and server to server; work closely with your instructor and Webmaster to perform this process successfully. Regardless of the method you choose, be sure to follow your instructor's directions and requirements.

GLOSSARY OF MLA MANUSCRIPT STYLE

The alphabetical glossary that follows answers most of your miscellaneous questions about matters of form, such as margins, pagination, dates, and numbers. For matters not addressed below, consult the index, which directs you to appropriate pages elsewhere in this text.

Abbreviations

Employ abbreviations often and consistently in notes and citations, but avoid them in the text. In your citations, but not in your text, always abbreviate these items:

- technical terms and reference words (anon., e.g., diss.)
- institutions (acad., assn., Cong.)
- dates (Jan., Feb.)
- states and countries (OH, CA, U.S.A.)
- names of publishers (McGraw, UP of Florida)
- titles of literary works (*Ado* for *Much Ado about Nothing*)
- Books of the Bible (Exod. For Exodus)

Accent Marks

When you quote, reproduce accents exactly as they appear in the original.

```
"La tradición clásica en españa," according to
Romana, remains strong in public school instruction
(16).
```

Ampersand

Avoid using the ampersand symbol "&" unless custom demands it, as in the John Updike story title "A & P."

Arabic Numerals

Arabic numerals should be used whenever possible: for volumes, books, parts, and chapters of works; acts, scenes, and lines of plays; cantos, stanzas, and lines of poetry.

Numbers Expressed as Figures in Your Text   Use figures in your text according to the following examples:

- All numbers 10 and above
- Numbers that represent ages, dates, time, size, score, amounts of money, and numerals used as numerals
- Statistical and mathematical numbers
- Numbers that precede units of measurement
- Numbers below 10 grouped with higher numbers

Number Use with Symbols   Use numerals with appropriate symbols (3%, $5.60); otherwise, use numerals only when the number cannot be spelled out in one or two words:

one hundred percent *but* 150 percent

a two-point average *but* a 2.5 average

one metric ton *but* 0.907 metric ton or 3.115 metric tons

Numbers Expressed in Words in Your Text   Spell out numbers in the following instances:

- Numbers less than 10 that are not used as measurements
- Common fractions
- Any number that begins a sentence
- References to centuries

Numbers as Both Words and Figures   Combine words and figures in these situations:

- Back-to-back modifiers:

  twelve 6-year-olds *or* 12 six-year-olds, *but not* 12 6-year olds

- Large numbers

  an operating budget of 4 million

Bullets, Numbers, and Indented Lists

Computers supply several bullet and number list styles whose indented lines begin with a circle, square, diamond, triangle, number, or letter. Use this feature for a list:

```
Observation 1: Kindergarten class
Observation 2: First grade class
Observation 3: Second grade class
```

Capitalization

For books, journals, magazines, and newspapers capitalize the first word, the last word, and all principal words, including words that follow hyphens in compound terms (e.g., French-Speaking Islands). Do not capitalize articles, prepositions that introduce phrases, conjunctions, and the *to* in infinitives when these words occur in the middle of the title (for example, *The Last of the Mohicans*). Following are some other instances for correctly employing capitalization:

- Capitalize the first word after the colon when introducing a rule, maxim, or principle and when introducing a quotation that is independent of your main sentence.

- When introducing a list or an elaboration on the idea of the first clause, do not capitalize the first word after the colon.

- Use capitals for trade names: Pepsi, Plexiglass, Nikon.

- Capitalize proper names used as adjectives but not the words used with them: Einstein's theory, Salk's vaccine.

- Capitalize the specific names of departments or courses, but use lowercase when they are used in a general sense: Department of Psychology *but* the psychology department

- Capitalize a noun that denotes a specific place in a numbered series but not nouns that name common parts of books: During `Test 6 we observed Group C, as shown on page 234.`

Comma

Use commas between items listed in a series of three or more, including before the *and* and *or* that precedes the last item. For example:

```
Reader (34), Scott (61), and Wellman (615-17) agree
with Steinbeck on this point.
```

Never use a comma and a dash together. The comma follows a parenthesis if your text requires the comma:

```
How should we order our lives, asks Thompson
(22-23), when we face "hostility from every
quarter"?
```

The comma goes inside single quotation marks as well as double quotation marks:

```
Such irony is discovered in Smith's article, "The
Sources of Franklin's 'The Ephemera,'" but not in
most textual discussions.
```

Figures and Tables

A table is a systematic presentation of materials, usually in columns. A figure is any nontext item that is not a table: blueprint, chart, diagram, drawing, graph, photo, photostat, map, and so on. A line graph serves a different purpose than a circle (pie) chart, and a bar graph plots different information than a scatter graph. Place captions above a table and below a figure. Here is an example:

| Table 1 | | | | |
Response by Class on Nuclear Energy Policy				
	Freshmen	Sophomores	Juniors	Seniors
1. More nuclear power	150	301	75	120
2. Less nuclear power	195	137	111	203
3. Present policy is				
acceptable	87	104	229	37

Sample table

Foreign Cities

In general, spell the names of foreign cities as they are written in original sources. However, for purposes of clarity, you may substitute an English name or provide both with one in parentheses:

    Köln (Cologne)   Braunschweig (Brunswick)

Indenting

Indent paragraphs five spaces or 1/2 inch. Indent block quotations (four lines or more) ten spaces or 1 inch from the left margin. If your block quotation is one paragraph, do not indent the first line more than the rest. However, if your block quotation is two or more paragraphs, indent the first line of each paragraph an extra three spaces or 1/4 inch. Use a five-space hanging indention for entries of the Works Cited page. (see Chapter 11, pages 183–185.)

Italics

If your word processing system and your printer will reproduce italic lettering, you may use it or underline titles and words that require emphasis (see also "Underscoring," 252–253, for a list).

Margins

A basic 1-inch margin on all sides of each page is recommended. Place your page number 1/2 inch below the top edge of the paper and 1 inch from the right edge. Your software has a ruler, menu, or style palette that allows you to set the margins. *Tip:* If you develop a header, the running head may appear 1 inch from the top, in which case your first line of text will begin 1 1/2 inches from the top.

Monetary Units

Spell out monetary amounts only if you can do so in three words or fewer. Conform to the following:

    $63 *or* sixty-three dollars

    $14.25 *but not* fourteen dollars and twenty-five cents

    $8 billion *or* eight billion dollars

    $10.3 billion *or* $10,300,000,000

Names of Persons

At the first mention of a person, give the full name (e.g., Ernest Hemingway or Margaret Mead) and thereafter give only the surname, such as Hemingway or Mead. Omit formal titles (Mr., Mrs., Dr., Hon.). Use simplified names of famous persons (e.g., Dante and Michelangelo) when they are familiar. Use pseudonyms (e.g., George Eliot, Mark Twain, Stendhal). Use fictional names (e.g., Huck, Lord Jim, Santiago, Captain Ahab).

Numbering Pages

Number your pages in a running head in the upper right-hand corner of each. Depending on the software, you can create the head with the Numbering or the Header feature. See the sample papers for page numbers for MLA style, pages 168–180.

Roman Numerals

Use capital roman numerals for titles of persons (Elizabeth II) and major sections of an outline (see pages 73–75). Use lowercase roman numerals for preliminary pages of text, as for a preface or introduction (iii, iv, v). Otherwise, use Arabic numerals (e.g., Vol. 5, Act 2, Ch. 17, Plate 21, 2 Sam. 2.1–8, or *Iliad* 2.121–30), *except* when writing for some instructors in history, philosophy, religion, music, art, and theater, in which case you may need to use roman numerals (e.g., III, Act II, I Sam. ii.1–8, *Hamlet* I.ii.5–6).

Running Heads

Repeat your last name in the upper right corner of every page just in front of the page number (see the sample paper, pages 168–180). APA style requires a short title with the page number.

Shortened Titles in the Text

Use abbreviated titles of books and articles mentioned often in the text after a first, full reference. For example, after its initial appearance, *Backgrounds to English as Language* should be shortened to *Backgrounds* in the text, notes, and in-text citations.

Spacing

As a general rule, double-space all typed material in your paper—the body, all indented quotations, and all Works Cited entries.

Space after punctuation according to these stipulations:

- Use one space after commas, semicolons, and colons.
- Use one space after punctuation marks at the end of sentences.
- Do not use a space before or after a dash.

Titles within Titles

For a book title that includes another title indicated by quotation marks, retain the quotation marks.

    O. Henry's Irony in "The Gift of the Magi"

For an article title within quotation marks that includes a book title, use italics or underlining for the book.

    "Great Expectations as a Novel of Initiation"

For an article title within quotation marks that includes another title indicated by quotation marks, enclose the shorter title in single quotation marks.

    "A Reading of O. Henry's 'The Gift of the Magi'"

For an underscored book title that incorporates another normally underscored title, do not underscore or italicize the shorter title nor place it within quotation marks.

    Interpretations of Great Expectations

Underscoring (Italicizing)
Titles

Use italics or underscoring for the titles of the following types of works:

Type of work	Example
book	*A Quaker Book of Wisdom*
bulletin	*Production Memo 3*
drama	*Desire under the Elms*

film	*Treasure of the Sierra Madre*
journal	*Journal of Sociology*
magazine	*Newsweek*
newspaper	*Boston Globe*
novel	*Band of Angels*
poem (book length)	*Idylls of the King*
short novel	*Billy Budd*

In contrast, place quotation marks around titles of articles, essays, chapters, sections, short poems, stories, songs, lectures, sermons, reports, and individual episodes of television programs.

Do not underscore the titles of sacred writings (Genesis, Old Testament); series (The New American Nation Series); editions (Variorum Edition of W. B. Yeats); societies (Victorian Society); courses (Greek Mythology); divisions of a work (preface, appendix, canto 3, scene 2); or descriptive phrases (Nixon's farewell address or Reagan's White House years).

Word Division
Avoid dividing words at the end of a line, even if it makes one line of text extremely short.

Credits

Index

Bold page numbers indicate areas of primary discussion.